Coaching Youth Gymnastics

American Sport Education Program
with USA Gymnastics

Human Kinetics

Library of Congress Cataloging-in-Publication Data

Coaching youth gymnastics / American Sport Education Program with USA Gymnastics.
   p. cm
 ISBN-13: 978-0-7360-8403-1 (soft cover)
 ISBN-10: 0-7360-8403-7 (soft cover)
 1. Gymnastics--Coaching--United States. I. American Sport Education Program. issuing body: II. USA Gymnastics. issuing body: III. Rookie coaches gymnastics guide. revision of:
 GV461.7.R66 2011
 796.440835--dc22

           2010045911

ISBN-10: 0-7360-8403-7 (print)
ISBN-13: 978-0-7360-8403-1 (print)

This book is a revised edition of *Rookie Coaches Gymnastics Guide*, published in 1993 by Human Kinetics, Inc. ("Welcome to Coaching" and Units 1-5); United States Gymnastics Federation (Units 6-8).

The Web addresses cited in this text were current as of December 2010 unless otherwise noted.

Content Providers: Kathy Feldmann, vice president of membership services at USA Gymnastics; Loree Galimore, director of club services at USA Gymnastics; Carisa Laughon, former director of educational services at USA Gymnastics; **Acquisitions Editors:** Annie Parrett and Aaron Thais; **Managing Editor:** Laura Podeschi; **Copyeditors:** Patricia MacDonald and Jan Feeney; **Permission Manager:** Martha Gullo; **Graphic Designer:** Nancy Rasmus; **Graphic Artist:** Francine Hamerski; **Cover Designer:** Keith Blomberg; **Photographer (cover):** © Human Kinetics; **Photographer (interior):** Neil Bernstein, unless otherwise noted; photos on pp. 9, 19, 31, 61, 95, 155, 177, 203, and 215 © USA Gymnastics; photos on pp. 1, 47, 73, and 135 © Human Kinetics; **Photo Asset Manager:** Laura Fitch; **Visual Production Assistant:** Joyce Brumfield; **Photo Production Manager:** Jason Allen; **Art Manager:** Kelly Hendren; **Associate Art Manager and Illustrator:** Alan L. Wilborn; **Printer:** Versa Press

We thank the Dana Mannix Gymnastics Center in Indianapolis, IN, for assistance in providing the location for the photo shoot for this book.

Copies of this book are available at special discounts for bulk purchase for sales promotions, premiums, fundraising, or educational use. Special editions or book excerpts can also be created to specifications. For details, contact the Special Sales Manager at Human Kinetics.

Printed in the United States of America   10 9 8 7 6 5 4 3 2

The paper in this book is certified under a sustainable forestry program.

Human Kinetics
Web site: www.HumanKinetics.com

United States: Human Kinetics
P.O. Box 5076
Champaign, IL 61825-5076
800-747-4457
e-mail: humank@hkusa.com

Canada: Human Kinetics
475 Devonshire Road Unit 100
Windsor, ON N8Y 2L5
800-465-7301 (in Canada only)
e-mail: info@hkcanada.com

Europe: Human Kinetics
107 Bradford Road
Stanningley
Leeds LS28 6AT, United Kingdom
+44 (0) 113 255 5665
e-mail: hk@hkeurope.com

Australia: Human Kinetics
57A Price Avenue
Lower Mitcham
South Australia 5062
08 8372 0999
e-mail: info@hkaustralia.com

New Zealand: Human Kinetics
P.O. Box 80
Torrens Park
South Australia 5062
0800 222 062
e-mail: info@hknewzealand.com

E4869

To anyone who has ever performed cartwheels, who once dreamed of performing cartwheels, or who appreciates and applauds all those who perform cartwheels.

Contents

GYMNASTICS

Welcome to Coaching

Coaching young people is an exciting way to be involved in sport. But it isn't easy. Some coaches are overwhelmed by the responsibilities involved in helping athletes through their early sport experiences. And that's not surprising because coaching youngsters requires more than just showing up. It also involves preparing them physically and mentally to compete effectively, fairly, and safely in their sport and providing them with a positive role model.

This book will help you meet the challenges so you can experience the many rewards of coaching young gymnasts. You'll learn how to meet your responsibilities as a coach, communicate well, provide for safety, and teach gymnastics skills while keeping them fun. More than 175 skills are included throughout the text to help you with your practices. Sample practice and season plans are also provided to guide you throughout your season.

If you would like more information about this or other ASEP resources, please contact us at the following address:

ASEP
P.O. Box 5076
Champaign, IL 61825-5076
800-747-5698
www.ASEP.com

Welcome From USA Gymnastics

Dear coach, instructor, or teacher,

On behalf of USA Gymnastics, welcome to *Coaching Youth Gymnastics.* It is one of many resources available to you through the American Sport Education Program (ASEP) and USA Gymnastics. Whether you want to learn how to teach proper fundamental skills or how to communicate better, this book can guide you through your experience of coaching youth gymnastics. It is a must-read for novice as well as experienced gymnastics teachers. Continuing education is important to everyone's growth and development.

You will find activities and plenty of resources to aid you in your coaching journey. These coaching methods are based on our experiences in teaching the many coaches and instructors of USA Gymnastics. Well-established resources such as *Rookie Coaches Gymnastics Guide, Sequential Gymnastics, Gymnastics Risk Management: Safety Course Handbook,* and *The Women's Level 1-4 Development Book* were used for this project.

This book is a great resource full of ideas to get you through your gymnastics classes. It establishes the important basics that all gymnastics participants must master. You will find it easy to follow—an excellent introduction to coaching youth gymnastics. Between ASEP and USA Gymnastics, you will have access to a wealth of practical information on coaching and teaching.

Your participation as a teacher and coach will have a profound impact on the gymnasts you influence, both today and for many years to come. On behalf of the athletes, thank you for coaching youth gymnastics.

For USA Gymnastics,

Kathy Feldmann, vice president of member services

Loree Galimore, director of club services

Carisa Laughon, former director of educational services

USA Gymnastics

132 E. Washington St., Suite 700

Indianapolis, IN 46204

800-345-4719

www.usagym.org

Foreword

Youth gymnastics coaches and instructors are the backbone of the sport. The highly technical demands of performing each event and the rigorous physical conditioning to support performance require proper guidance from a capable mentor.

Knowledge of the sport and an ability to teach it are essential, but equally important are coaches' philosophy, communication skills, level of organization, concern for safety, and supportive demeanor. That's why I encourage you to read and apply the material in *Coaching Youth Gymnastics* to your work.

Like me, most gymnasts start at a very early age. Few will have the good fortune to compete and win medals at the world championships and Olympics, but that does not make their experience any less significant. Not only do gymnasts learn flexibility, strength, balance, and body awareness, but they also learn important life lessons such as goal setting, perseverance, and dedication. Young gymnasts need and deserve coaches who emphasize children's overall development as athletes and as people, not just how high they can climb in the competitive ranks.

Most observers might focus on my competitive successes, but I also had my share of setbacks and injuries. I faced those obstacles with a strong inner drive to excel and the support of my coaches and family.

I applaud USA Gymnastics for all of their coaching education efforts and recommend that you take advantage of every learning opportunity, starting with this book. Not only will you be better prepared to coach effectively, but the young gymnasts under your tutelage will have the great experience they seek and deserve in this incredible sport.

Shannon Miller
Seven-time Olympic medalist and nine-time world medalist
United States' most decorated gymnast

Skill Finder

> continued

> continued

> *continued*

> continued

> continued

Stepping Into Coaching

In the sport of gymnastics, the titles of *coach* and *instructor* are typically used to mean different things. Instructors generally teach students who participate in gymnastics at a preschool or recreational level, while coaches instruct, guide, and prepare athletes for gymnastics competition. Yet the basic task of both gymnastics coaches and instructors is to teach and help gymnasts learn. So although the term *coach* is used most frequently throughout this book, much of the material can apply to both coaches and instructors.

If you are like most gymnastics coaches, you have probably been recruited from the ranks of former gymnasts, gymnastics enthusiasts, coaches of similar sports, or even parents. Like many rookie and veteran coaches, you probably have had little formal instruction on coaching. But when the call from the local gymnastics club went out for coaches, you answered because you like children and enjoy gymnastics and perhaps because you want to be involved in a worthwhile activity.

Your initial coaching assignment may be difficult. You may not know everything there is to know about gymnastics or about how to work with children. *Coaching Youth Gymnastics* presents the basics of coaching gymnastics effectively. To start, we look at your responsibilities and what's involved in being a coach. We also examine five tools for being an effective coach.

Your Responsibilities as a Coach

Coaching at any level involves much more than just teaching a cartwheel or spotting a back salto. Coaching involves accepting the tremendous responsibility you face when parents put their children in your care. As a gymnastics coach, you'll be called on to do the following:

1. **Provide a safe physical environment.**

Participating in gymnastics involves inherent risks. As a coach you're responsible for minimizing risk, and one way to do this is to conduct regular inspections of facilities, apparatus, and equipment used for practice and competition (see "Sample Facility Inspection Form" on page 241 of the appendix). Providing a safe physical environment also includes offering proper supervision and instruction, educating the gymnasts regarding safety policies (see "Coaches' Safety Checklist" on page 236 of the appendix), removing or preventing known hazards, ensuring access to first aid supplies, and having an emergency action plan in place (see page 37 of chapter 4 for more information).

2. **Communicate in a positive way.**

As you already know, you have a lot to communicate. You'll communicate not only with your athletes and their parents but also with fellow coaches, officials, administrators, and others. Communicate in a positive way that demonstrates you have the best interests of the gymnasts at heart (see chapter 2 for more information).

3. Teach the fundamental skills of gymnastics.

When teaching the fundamental skills of gymnastics, keep in mind that you want to make sure your gymnasts are always having fun. Therefore, we ask that you help all athletes be the best they can be by creating a fun yet productive practice environment (see chapter 5 for more information). Additionally, to help your young gymnasts improve their skills, you need to have a sound understanding of gymnastics skills, progressions, and technique. You should reassure gymnasts and parents that you will be teaching the safest techniques in order to help gymnasts prevent injury.

4. Teach the rules of gymnastics.

Introduce the rules of gymnastics, and incorporate them into individual instruction (see chapter 3 for more information). Many rules can be taught in practice, including aspects of judging, proper skill execution and penalties, and general gymnastics etiquette. Plan to review the rules any time an opportunity naturally arises in practices.

5. Direct athletes in competition.

Your responsibilities may include determining readiness for competition, determining appropriate levels of competition, relating appropriately to officials and opposing coaches and gymnasts, and making sound decisions during meets (see chapter 12 for more information on coaching during meets). Remember that the focus is not on winning at all costs but on coaching your kids to compete well, do their best, improve their gymnastics skills, and strive to win within the rules.

6. Help your athletes become fit and value fitness for a lifetime.

We want you to help your athletes become fit so they can participate in gymnastics safely and successfully. We also want your gymnasts to learn to become fit on their own, understand the value of fitness, and enjoy training. Thus, we ask you not to use conditioning (e.g., doing push-ups or running laps) as a form of punishment. Make it fun to get fit, and make it fun to participate in gymnastics so that your athletes will stay fit for a lifetime.

7. Help young people develop character.

Character development includes learning, caring, being honest and respectful, and taking responsibility. These intangible qualities are no less important to teach than the skill of a handstand. We ask you to teach these values to athletes by demonstrating and encouraging behaviors that express these values at all times. For example, stress to young gymnasts the importance of encouraging their teammates, competing within the rules, and showing respect for their opponents. Be a positive role model for your gymnasts.

These are your responsibilities as a coach. Remember that every athlete is an individual. You must provide a wholesome environment in which every athlete has the opportunity to learn without fear while having fun and enjoying the overall gymnastics experience.

Five Tools of an Effective Coach

You most likely already have the traditional coaching tools—such as appropriate clothing and a clipboard. They'll help you in the act of coaching, but to be successful, you'll need five other tools that cannot be bought. These tools are available only through self-examination and hard work; they're easy to remember with the acronym COACH:

C	Comprehension
O	Outlook
A	Affection
C	Character
H	Humor

Comprehension

Comprehension of the rules and skills of gymnastics is required. You must understand the elements of the sport. To improve your comprehension of gymnastics, take the following steps:

- Read about the rules of gymnastics in chapter 3 of this book. USA Gymnastics also publishes rules, compulsory elements and exercises, and requirements for optional exercises according to discipline in their *Junior Olympic Code of Points* and *Rules and Policies.* These resources are available at www.usagym.org.
- Read about the fundamental skills of gymnastics in chapters 7 through 11.
- Read additional gymnastics coaching books, including those available from the American Sport Education Program (ASEP), Human Kinetics, and USA Gymnastics.
- Take coaching education courses, and attend gymnastics coaching clinics and workshops (many are available through USA Gymnastics).
- Contact youth gymnastics organizations, including USA Gymnastics (www.usagym.org).
- Find a mentor—talk with more experienced coaches.
- Observe local youth, college, and high school gymnastics events.
- Watch gymnastics events on television.

COACHING TIP Attending local gymnastics events is a low-cost way not only for you to improve your knowledge of the sport but also for gymnasts of all ages to observe the skills of gymnastics. Consider working with your gymnasts' parents to organize a team outing to a local event in place of or as a complement to a weekend practice.

In addition to having gymnastics knowledge, you must implement proper training and safety methods so that your gymnasts can participate with lower risk of injury. Even then, injuries may occur. More often than not, you'll be the first person responding to your athletes' injuries, so be sure you understand the basic emergency care procedures described in chapter 4. Also, read in that chapter how to handle more serious sport injury situations.

Outlook

The second coaching tool refers to your perspective and goals—what you seek as a coach. The most common coaching objectives are to have fun; to help athletes develop their physical, mental, and social skills; and to strive to win. Thus, your outlook involves your priorities, your planning, and your vision for the future. See "Assessing Your Priorities" on page 6 to learn more about the priorities you set for yourself as a coach.

ASEP has a motto that will help you keep your outlook in line with the best interests of the kids on your team. It summarizes in four words all you need to remember when establishing your coaching priorities:

Athletes first, winning second.

This motto recognizes that striving to win is an important, even vital, part of sports. But it emphatically states that no efforts in striving to win should be made at the expense of the athletes' well-being, development, and enjoyment. Take the following actions to better define your outlook:

- With the members of your coaching staff, determine your priorities for the season.
- Prepare for situations that may challenge your priorities.
- Set goals for yourself and your gymnasts that are consistent with your priorities.
- Plan how you and your gymnasts can best attain your goals.
- Review your goals frequently to be sure you are staying on track.

Assessing Your Priorities

Even though all coaches focus on competition, we want you to focus on *positive* competition—keeping the pursuit of victory in perspective by making decisions that, first, are in the best interests of the athletes and, second, will help them succeed.

So, how do you know if your outlook and priorities are in order? Here's a little test:

1. Which situation would you be most proud of?
   a. *knowing that each participant enjoys participating in gymnastics*
   b. *seeing that all athletes improve their gymnastics skills*
   c. *watching your gymnasts win championships*
2. Which statement best reflects your thoughts about sport?
   a. *If it isn't fun, don't do it.*
   b. *Everyone should learn something every day.*
   c. *Sport isn't fun if you don't win.*
3. How would you like your gymnasts to remember you?
   a. *as a coach who was fun*
   b. *as a coach who provided a good base of fundamental skills*
   c. *as a coach who helped them win*
4. Which would you most like to hear a parent of an athlete on your team say?
   a. *Nicole really had a good time participating in gymnastics this year.*
   b. *Josh learned some important lessons participating in gymnastics this year.*
   c. *Megan won every gymnastics competition this year.*
5. Which of the following would be the most rewarding moment of your season?
   a. *having your team want to continue practicing, even after practice is over*
   b. *seeing one of your gymnasts finally master her glide kip on bars*
   c. *watching one of your gymnasts qualify for the national meet*

Look over your answers. If you most often selected *a* responses, then having fun is most important to you. A majority of *b* answers suggest that skill development is what attracts you to coaching. And if *c* was your most frequent response, winning is tops on your list of coaching priorities. If your priorities are in order, your athletes' well-being will take precedence over your team's success every time.

Affection

Another vital tool you will want to have in your coaching kit is a genuine concern for the young people you coach. This requires having a passion for kids, a desire to share with them your enjoyment and knowledge of gymnastics, and the patience and understanding that allow all of your gymnasts to grow from their involvement in sport. You can demonstrate your affection and patience in many ways, including the following:

- Make an effort to get to know each athlete on your team.
- Treat each athlete as an individual.
- Empathize with athletes trying to learn new and difficult skills.
- Treat athletes as you would like to be treated under similar circumstances.
- Control your emotions.
- Show your enthusiasm for being involved with your team.
- Keep an upbeat tempo and a positive tone in all of your communications.

Character

The fact that you have decided to coach young gymnasts probably means you think participation in sport is important. But whether or not that participation develops character in your athletes depends as much on you as it does on the sport itself. How can you help your gymnasts build character?

To teach kids good character, coaches must model appropriate behaviors for sport and life. That means more than just saying the right things. What you say and what you do must match. There is no place in coaching for the "Do as I say, not as I do" philosophy. Challenge, support, encourage, and reward every youngster, and your gymnasts will be more likely to accept—even celebrate—their differences. Be in control before, during, and after all practices and competitions. And don't be afraid to admit that you were wrong. No one is perfect!

Each member of your coaching staff should consider the following steps to becoming a good role model:

- Take stock of your strengths and weaknesses.
- Build on your strengths.
- Set goals for yourself to improve on those areas that you would not want your athletes to copy.
- If you slip up, apologize to your team and to yourself. You'll do better next time.

Humor

Humor is an often-overlooked coaching tool. It means having the ability to laugh at yourself and with your athletes during practices and competitions. Nothing helps balance the seriousness of a skill session like a chuckle or two. And a sense of humor puts in perspective the many mistakes your gymnasts will make. So don't get upset over every bent leg or respond negatively to a fall. Allow yourself and your athletes to enjoy the ups, and don't dwell on the downs. Here are some tips for injecting humor and fun into your practices:

- Make practices fun by including a variety of activities.
- Keep all athletes involved during practice.
- Consider laughter by your athletes to be a sign of enjoyment, not of waning discipline.
- Smile!

Communicating as a Coach

2

COMMUNICAT

In chapter 1, you learned about the tools you need for coaching: comprehension, outlook, affection, character, and humor. These are essentials for effective coaching; without them, you'd have a difficult time getting started. But none of the tools will work if you don't know how to use them with your gymnasts—and this requires skillful communication. This chapter examines what communication is and how you can become a more effective communicator.

Coaches often mistakenly believe that communication occurs only when instructing athletes to do something, but verbal commands are just a small part of the communication process. More than half of the communication between people is nonverbal. So when you are coaching, remember that actions speak louder than words.

Communication in its simplest form involves two people: a sender and a receiver. The sender transmits the message verbally, through facial expressions, and sometimes through body language. Once the message is sent, the receiver must receive it and, optimally, understand it. A receiver who fails to pay attention will miss part, if not all, of the message.

Sending Effective Messages

Young athletes often have little understanding of the rules and skills of gymnastics and probably even less confidence in their ability to perform. So they need accurate, understandable, and supportive messages to help them along. That's why your verbal and nonverbal messages are important.

Verbal Messages

"Sticks and stones may break my bones, but words will never hurt me" isn't true. Spoken words can have a strong and long-lasting effect. And coaches' words are particularly influential because youngsters place great importance on what coaches say. Perhaps you, like many former youth sport participants, have a difficult time remembering much of anything your elementary school teachers told you, but you can probably still recall several specific things your coaches at that level said. Such is the lasting effect of a coach's comments to an athlete.

Whether you are correcting misbehavior, teaching proper technique for a back handspring, or praising one of your gymnasts for good effort, you should consider a number of things when sending a message verbally:

- Be positive and honest.
- Speak clearly and simply.
- Say it loud enough, and then say it again.
- Be consistent.

Be Positive and Honest

Nothing turns people off like hearing someone nag all the time, and athletes react similarly to a coach who gripes constantly. Kids particularly need encouragement because they often doubt their ability to perform in a sport. So look for and tell your gymnasts what they have done well.

However, don't cover up poor or incorrect technique with rosy words of praise. Kids know all too well when they've erred, and no cheerfully expressed cliche can undo their mistakes. If you fail to acknowledge errors, your athletes will think you are a phony.

An effective way to correct a performance error is to first point out the part of the skill that the gymnast has performed correctly. Then explain—in a positive manner—the error that the gymnast has made, and show her the correct way to do it. Finish by encouraging the gymnast and emphasizing the correct technique.

Make sure you don't follow a positive statement with the word *but*. For example, you shouldn't say, "You kept your head in well, Kelly, but your legs are still bent in your handstand." Many kids will ignore the positive statement and focus on the negative one. Instead, you could say, "You kept your head in well on your handstand, Kelly. And if you focus on straightening your legs, it will be beautiful. Way to go."

Speak Clearly and Simply

Positive and honest messages are most effective when expressed directly in words your gymnasts understand. Beating around the bush is ineffective and inefficient. And if you ramble, your gymnasts will miss the point of your message and probably lose interest. Here are some tips for saying things clearly:

- Organize your thoughts before speaking to your athletes.
- Know your subject as completely as possible.
- Explain things thoroughly, but don't bore your athletes with long-winded monologues.
- Use language your athletes can understand, and be consistent in your terminology. However, avoid trying to be hip by using their age group's slang.

Say It Loud Enough, and Then Say It Again

Talk to your team in a voice that all members can hear. A crisp, vigorous voice commands attention and respect; garbled and weak speech is tuned out. It's okay and, in fact, appropriate to soften your voice when speaking to a gymnast individually about a personal problem. But most of the time your messages will be for all of your athletes to hear, so make sure they can. An enthusiastic voice also motivates athletes and tells them that you enjoy being their coach. A word of caution, however: Avoid dominating the setting with a booming voice that distracts attention from athletes' performances.

Sometimes what you say, even if stated loudly and clearly, won't sink in the first time. This may be particularly true when young gymnasts hear words they don't understand. To avoid boring repetition and still get your message across, you can say the same thing in a slightly different way. For instance, when explaining a drill, you might first tell your gymnasts, "Use your arms!" If the gymnasts don't appear to understand, you might say, "Arms by your ears!" The second form of the message may get through to gymnasts who missed it the first time around.

COACHING TIP Remember, terms that you are familiar with and understand may be completely foreign to your gymnasts, especially younger children or beginners. Adjust your vocabulary to match the age group. Although 12- to 14-year-olds may understand expressions such as "drive your heels" or "keep your legs tight," 8- and 9-year-olds may be confused by this terminology. In some cases, you may need to use demonstrations with the gymnasts so they can "see" the term and how it relates to gymnastics.

Be Consistent

People often say things in ways that imply a different message. For example, a touch of sarcasm added to "Way to go!" sends an entirely different message than the words themselves suggest. You should avoid sending mixed messages. Keep the tone of your voice consistent with the words you use. And don't say something one day and contradict it the next; athletes will get their wires crossed.

You also want to keep your terminology consistent. Many gymnastics terms describe the same or similar skills. Take one popular skill, for example: One coach may use the term *back extension roll* to refer to this move, while another coach may use *back roll to handstand*. Although both might be correct, to be consistent as a staff, the coaches of a team should agree on all terms before the start of the season and then stay with them.

Nonverbal Messages

Just as you should be consistent in the tone of voice and words you use, you should also keep your verbal and nonverbal messages consistent. An extreme example of failing to do this is shaking your head, indicating disapproval, while at the same time telling an athlete "Nice try." Which is the athlete to believe, your gesture or your words?

Messages can be sent nonverbally in several ways. Facial expressions and body language are just two of the more obvious forms of nonverbal signals. Keep in mind that as a coach you need to be a teacher first, and any action that detracts from the message you are trying to convey should be avoided.

Facial Expressions

The look on a person's face is the quickest clue to what the person thinks. Your gymnasts know this, so they will study your face, looking for a sign that will tell them more than the words you say. Don't try to fool them by putting on a happy or blank "mask." They'll see through it, and you'll lose credibility.

Serious, stone-faced expressions provide no cues to kids who want to know how they are performing. When faced with this, kids will just assume you're unhappy or disinterested. Don't be afraid to smile. A smile from a coach can give a great boost to an unsure athlete. Plus, a smile lets your gymnasts know you are happy to be coaching them. But don't overdo it, or your gymnasts won't be able to tell when you are genuinely pleased by something they've done or when you are just putting on a smiling face.

Body Language

What would your gymnasts think you were feeling if you came to practice slouched over, with your head down and your shoulders slumped? Would they think you were tired, bored, or unhappy? What would they think you were feeling if you watched them during a competition with your hands on your hips, your jaws clenched, and your face reddened? Would they think you were upset with them, disgusted at an official, or mad at a fan? Probably some or all of these things would enter your gymnasts' minds. And none is the impression you want your gymnasts to have of you. That's why you should carry yourself in a pleasant, confident, and vigorous manner.

COACHING TIP   As a coach, you need to be aware of your body language. Athletes of all ages will pick up on your actions and habits, so you must be sure to provide a good example for your gymnasts to model. All it takes is a few eye rolls or wild hand gestures to send a message that this type of behavior is acceptable, even if that is not your intent.

Physical contact can also be a very important use of body language. A high five, a pat on the head, and an arm around the shoulder are effective ways to show approval, concern, affection, and joy to your gymnasts. Youngsters are especially in need of this type of nonverbal message. Keep within the obvious moral and legal limits, of course, but don't be reluctant to show your gymnasts that you care through appropriate physical contact, sending a message that can be expressed only in this way. Remember, a high five is always acceptable and appropriate.

Improving Your Receiving Skills

Now let's examine the other half of the communication process: receiving messages. Too often, very good senders are very poor receivers of messages. But as a coach of young athletes, you must be able to fulfill both roles effectively.

The requirements for receiving messages are simple, but receiving skills are perhaps less satisfying and therefore underdeveloped compared with sending skills. People seem to enjoy hearing themselves talk more than they enjoy hearing others talk. But if you learn the keys to receiving messages and make a strong effort to use them with your athletes, you'll be surprised by what you've been missing.

Pay Attention

First, you must pay attention; you must want to hear what others need to communicate to you. That's not always easy when you're busy coaching and have many things competing for your attention. But in one-on-one or team meetings with athletes, you must focus on what they are telling you, both verbally and nonverbally. You'll be amazed at the little signals you pick up. This focused attention will not only help you catch every word your gymnasts say but also enable you to notice your gymnasts' moods and physical states. In addition, you'll get an idea of your gymnasts' feelings toward you and other gymnasts on the team.

Listen Carefully

How you receive a message from another person, perhaps more than anything else you do, demonstrates how much you care for the sender and what that person has to tell you. If you care little for your athletes or have little regard for what they have to say, it will show in how you attend and listen to them. You need to check yourself. Do you find your mind wandering to what you are going to do after practice while one of your gymnasts is talking to you? Do you frequently have to ask your athletes, "What did you say?" If so, you need to work on your receiving mechanics of attending and listening. But if you find that you're missing the messages your athletes send, perhaps the most critical question you should ask yourself is this: "Do I care enough to be a coach?"

Providing Feedback

So far we've discussed separately the sending and receiving of messages. But we all know that senders and receivers switch roles several times during an interaction. One person initiates communication by sending a message to another person, who then receives the message. The receiver then becomes the sender by responding to the person who sent the initial message. These verbal and nonverbal responses are called *feedback*.

Your gymnasts will look to you for feedback all the time. They will want to know how you think they are performing, what you think of their ideas, and whether their efforts please you. You can respond in many different ways, and how you respond will strongly affect your gymnasts. They will react most favorably to positive feedback.

Praising gymnasts when they have performed or behaved well is an effective way to get them to repeat (or try to repeat) that behavior. And positive feedback for effort is an especially effective way to motivate youngsters to work on difficult skills. So rather than shouting at and providing negative feedback to gymnasts who have made mistakes, you should try offering positive feedback and letting them know what they did correctly and how they can improve. Sometimes just the way you word feedback can make it more positive than negative. For example, instead of saying, "Don't take steps on your landing," you might say, "Land with your legs slightly bent, chest up, and arms level with your heart." Then your gymnasts will be focusing on what to do instead of what not to do.

Positive feedback can be verbal or nonverbal. Telling young athletes, especially in front of teammates, that they have performed well is a great way to boost their confidence. And a pat on the back or a high five communicates that you recognize a gymnast's performance.

Communicating With Other Groups

In addition to sending and receiving messages and providing proper feedback to athletes, coaching also involves interacting with members of the coaching staff, parents, fans, officials, and opposing coaches. If you don't communicate effectively with these groups, your coaching career will be unpleasant and short-lived. So try the following suggestions for communicating with these groups.

Coaching Staff

Before you hold your first practice, the coaching staff should meet and discuss the roles and responsibilities that each coach will undertake during the year. Depending on the number of coaches, the staff responsibilities can be divided into different areas. For example, one coach may be in charge of working with the gymnasts on vault and bars, while another may be responsible for beam and floor. The head coach has the final responsibility for the team, but the assistant coaches should be responsible for their areas as much as possible.

Before the season starts, the coaching staff must also discuss and agree on terminology, plans for practices, meet-day organization, the method of communicating during practices and competitions, and event schedules. The coaches on your staff must present a united front and speak with one voice, and they must all take a similar approach to coaching, interacting with the gymnasts and parents, and interacting with one another. Disagreements should be discussed away from the gym, and each coach should have a say as the staff members come to an agreement.

COACHING TIP Although all the coaches on your staff need to share similar coaching philosophies and be able to work together, not all coaches have to be identical. On the contrary, you should look for coaches who can complement your weak areas. For example, perhaps you're confident in your ability to teach tumbling skills, but you're not as comfortable with the nuances of jumps, leaps, and choreography. In addition, maybe you sometimes struggle with handling all the logistics of preparing the team for competition or notifying parents and athletes of last-minute schedule changes. In this situation, you should consider recruiting other coaches (or parents) who can take over these kinds of responsibilities.

Parents

An athlete's parents need to be assured that their son or daughter is under the direction of a coach who is both knowledgeable about the sport and concerned about the youngster's well-being. You can put their worries to rest by holding a preseason parent orientation meeting in which you describe your background and your approach to coaching as well as provide expectations for the season. See "Preseason Meeting Topics" on the following page for a sample outline of information to cover at a parent orientation meeting. (Note that the type of paperwork needed before the season starts, as well as various procedures and costs, will vary by team.)

If parents contact you with a concern during the season, you should listen to them closely and try to offer positive responses. If you need to communicate with parents, you can catch them after a practice or meet, give them a phone call, or send a note through e-mail or regular mail. Messages sent to parents through athletes are too often lost, misinterpreted, or forgotten.

Fans

There may be times when you hear criticism of your coaching coming from parents, fans, or others. When you hear something negative about the job you're doing, keep calm, consider whether the message has any value, and if not, forget it. If the message does have value, you should reflect on the comment and then determine positive steps that you can take to improve in that area. Acknowledging critical, unwarranted comments from a parent or fan during a meet will only encourage others to voice their opinions. Instead, communicate to fans through your actions that you are a confident, competent coach.

You should also prepare your gymnasts for criticisms from competitors, fans, parents, and others. Tell your gymnasts that it is you, not the spectators, whom they should listen to. If you notice that one of your gymnasts is rattled by a comment, you should reassure her that your evaluation is more objective and favorable—and the one that counts.

Preseason Meeting Topics

1. Share your coaching philosophy.
2. Outline the paperwork that is needed, such as the following:
   - Medical history form or preparticipation physical exam
   - Participation registration form with waiver and release (see page 247 of the appendix)
   - Consent to treatment form (see page 251 of the appendix)
   - Emergency information card (see page 252 of the appendix)
3. Go over the inherent risks of gymnastics and other safety issues. Explain safety rules and policies. Review your emergency action plan (see page 37 of chapter 4).
4. Inform parents of procedures related to team warm-ups, leotards, and other equipment, including what items the club will provide and what the gymnasts must furnish themselves.
5. Go over the proper attire that should be worn at each practice session as well as for competitions.
6. Review the season practice and competition schedule, including the date, location, and time of each practice and meet (when available).
7. Discuss nutrition, hydration, and rest for gymnasts.
8. Explain the goals for the team.
9. Cover methods of communication: e-mail list, emergency phone numbers, interactive Web site, and so on.
10. Discuss ways that parents can help with the team.
11. Discuss standards of conduct for coaches, gymnasts, and parents.
12. Provide time for questions and answers.

Officials

How you communicate with officials will have a great influence on the way your gymnasts behave toward them. Therefore, you must set a good example. Greet officials with a handshake, an introduction, and perhaps casual conversation about the upcoming competition. Indicate your respect for them before, during, and after the events. Don't shout, make nasty remarks, or use disrespectful body gestures. Your gymnasts will see your actions and get the idea that such behavior is appropriate. Plus, if the official hears or sees you, the communication between the two of you will break down.

If you disagree with a score, there are often inquiry procedures that can be initiated. Additionally, many judges may be willing to provide clarification and feedback to you at the appropriate time after a competition. It is important not to blame the judges for low scores. Rather, work to figure out the deductions, and focus on making improvements in your gymnasts' performances.

Opposing Coaches

Make an effort to visit with coaches of the opposing teams before the competition. During the meet, don't get into a personal feud with another coach. Remember, the kids, not the coaches, are competing. And by getting along well with the opposing coaches, you'll show your gymnasts that competition involves cooperation. You can portray good sportsmanship by showing respect for other coaches even if you are not friends with them away from the gym.

Understanding Rules, Apparatus, and Equipment

3

The objectives of gymnastics are simple: Perform each skill or routine with the fewest technical errors and the greatest amount of artistic impression. Of course, this is much easier said than done.

The number of skills in each of the four events for women's artistic gymnastics and six events for men's artistic gymnastics can make things tough on new coaches, who might feel overwhelmed at first. This introduction to the basic rules of gymnastics won't cover every rule of the sport but instead will give you a general understanding of the USA Gymnastics Junior Olympic Program. In this chapter, we cover the basics of the sport for the women's and men's artistic disciplines, including a program overview, apparatus and equipment, and attire. We also describe specifics such as competition etiquette and rules of competition, and then we wrap things up with some officiating basics.

Junior Olympic Program

USA Gymnastics developed its Junior Olympic Program to provide skill development opportunities and progressive competition levels for participants. The structure of the program allows gymnasts to develop a foundation of basic skills and safely advance from the beginner level through advanced levels of competition and potentially into the elite (Olympic-level) program.

Complete program objectives, rules, and requirements are provided in each program's *Rules and Policies* handbook and the Junior Olympic competition manuals, available through www.usagym.org. Consult these resources for the most complete and up-to-date information.

Age Requirements for Gymnastics

Before we begin, let's discuss why age requirements are defined. Strict age requirements, especially regarding the minimum age of participation, are in place within the USA Gymnastics Junior Olympic Program for safety reasons. Many skills require significant strength, power, and flexibility and are more safely performed by school-age and older athletes. The bodies of preschool children are often not developed enough to safely perform certain skills or withstand the repetition required for competition preparation. Skill progressions and drills can be used with preschool gymnasts to help them develop physically and prepare for the competitive program. For specific age requirements, consult the USA Gymnastics *Rules and Policies* manual for the respective discipline.

Apparatus and Equipment

Apparatus is the term for items used directly for competition. *Equipment* generally refers to any items in the gym outside of those used directly for competition. An example of an apparatus is a set of uneven bars. Additional mats, such as trapezoids, and spotting belts would be considered equipment.

You might be lucky enough to have access to the latest state-of-the-art gymnastics apparatus in your facility. Or maybe your team uses older apparatus and equipment that are still in good condition. Regardless, you can teach your athletes the fundamental skills of gymnastics. You just need to ensure that the gymnasts have a safe place to practice and compete, the apparatus and equipment are inspected frequently and well maintained, and the gymnastics area is free of obstacles.

The typical gymnastics center will have at least one of each of the competitive apparatus. General descriptions are provided here. For complete apparatus specifications and competition regulations, consult the USA Gymnastics *Rules and Policies* manual for the respective discipline.

Vault Table   The vaulting apparatus used in training and competition. Gymnasts run down a runway, jump off a springboard, push off the vaulting surface with their hands, and perform a skill in the air (ranging from a simple tuck position to multiple flips and twists) before landing on their feet. The runway is a clearly defined, narrow area consisting of a flat, uniform surface. The vault table is used for women's and men's artistic gymnastics.

Springboard   A device used for jumping or rebounding to gain height. It is typically used for vault and for mounts on uneven bars, parallel bars, and balance beam. A safety-zone mat must be placed snugly around the springboard for vaults with a round-off entry.

Uneven Bars   Consist of a low bar and high bar of fiberglass rails with wood covering. The bars run parallel to each other but at different heights. Gymnasts perform skills ranging from simple hip circles to intricate turns and release moves and are judged on their form and the level of difficulty of skills. In optional competition, gymnasts must perform skills on both bars and make a certain number of transitions between the low bar and the high bar. Routines end with a dismount onto the mat. Uneven bars are used in women's artistic gymnastics.

Balance Beam   Used in women's artistic gymnastics, the balance beam is 4 inches (10 cm) wide and 16 feet (4.9 m) long. It has a padded, sueded surface and is raised off the floor. Gymnasts perform tumbling, balance, and dance skills and are required to perform the skills in all directions and at various levels on the beam (i.e., down low on the beam as well as up high on their toes). Routines end with a dismount off the end or side of the beam.

Floor Exercise Area   A 40-by-40-foot (12 by 12 m) area. Most floor exercise areas consist of a carpeted surface covering thousands of springs and a foam layer. Gymnasts perform tumbling passes across the diagonal areas; women's floor exercise routines include dance combinations and jump series. This apparatus is used in women's and men's artistic gymnastics as well as acrobatic gymnastics. Women's floor routines are set to music.

Pommel Horse   An apparatus in men's artistic gymnastics. It is a traditional "horse" body placed horizontally on a base with two pommels attached on the top. Routines consist of swinging movements around and over the horse.

Gymnasts are expected to perform skills on each pommel as well as on each flat area of the horse. Dismounts involve relatively simple moves from the pommel horse to the mat.

Still Rings A men's artistic gymnastics apparatus formed by two circular rings suspended from a metal tower or frame. Gymnasts perform swinging skills, strength moves, and balance moves and end their routines with a dismount onto the mat.

Parallel Bars Consists of two wood rails of equal dimension and height running parallel to each other, just as the name suggests. Routines consist of swinging skills, static handstands, release moves, and strength moves. A routine ends with a dismount to the mat. This apparatus is used in men's artistic gymnastics.

Horizontal Bar A single bar rail raised above the floor. Also known as the high bar, horizontal bar is a men's artistic gymnastics event. Gymnasts perform swinging skills, handstands, turns, grip changes, and release moves. A routine ends with a dismount to the mat.

In addition to the standard gymnastics apparatus, other pieces and types of equipment can be very useful in the gym, especially to facilitate the skill-learning process. Helpful equipment may include the following:

Landing Mat A firm mat designed to absorb the force of a landing. This is the typical mat used under and around apparatus. Landing mats can be 4 inches to 8 inches (10 cm to 20 cm) in height. Note that mat specifications can change. It is important to review the most current edition of the USA Gymnastics *Rules and Policies* manual, which you can find online at www.usagym.org.

Trampoline
A rebound device that consists of a horizontal bed attached to a frame by springs. The bed can be made of various materials depending on the level of performance. The bed is approximately 14 feet (4.3 m) long by 7 feet (2.1 m) wide.

Tumbling Trampoline A long, narrow trampoline that is typically firmer than a traditional trampoline. A tumbling trampoline is not a competitive apparatus, but it is a useful piece of equipment for various drills and training exercises.

Panel Mat A basic vinyl-covered mat constructed of a single layer of resilient foam, ranging in thickness from 1 to 2 inches (2.5 to 5 cm), that can be folded into panels approximately 2 feet (.6 m) wide. Panel mats serve a variety of functions, acting as extra padding for landing surfaces and devices for training progressions and exercises.

Incline Mat A mat with a sloped surface, with one end taller than the other. Also known as a wedge mat, this type of mat is often used to help gymnasts learn rolls and can be an important piece of equipment for many other drills.

Trapezoid   A mat or set of mats in a trapezoid shape, commonly used in place of a vault table for younger and beginning gymnasts. It can also be used as a platform for the coach to stand on when spotting or as a piece of equipment for other activities in the gym.

Parallette   Equipment built to mimic a single bar or parallel bars. Horizontal bars are mounted on blocks that are close to the floor. This equipment is typically used for lead-up skills, for drills, and by younger gymnasts.

Skill Cushion   A mat that can be added to a landing area or under an apparatus to provide extra softness and absorbency for landings or falls. Skill cushions are generally 8 inches (20 cm) thick.

Sting Mat   A thin mat that can be used for dismounts and landings to provide extra absorbency. Sting mats are generally 1 inch (2.5 cm) thick.

Apparel

Rules exist for the type of attire to be worn at sanctioned competitions. Outside of the competitive setting, coaches should direct their athletes regarding proper attire. Monitoring the quality and fit of the clothes your gymnasts wear is a simple way to minimize potential injuries. Clothing should allow freedom of movement but not be so loose that it hinders safe performance. Following are some examples of proper apparel:

- For girls, leotards are best. Tights or nonbaggy shorts (ideally bike-type shorts) may also be worn.
- For boys, T-shirts and athletic shorts are recommended.
- Gymnasts should not wear clothing that is too baggy or has zippers, snaps, buckles, or strings. This type of clothing could interfere with a gymnast's ability to move safely, could get caught on the equipment, and could scratch or cut the gymnast or coach.
- Bare feet are best to avoid slipping on the floor or on equipment in the gym. Special gymnastics shoes are also appropriate to wear.
- Jewelry should not be worn.
- Longer hair should be tied back and secured away from the eyes.
- Fingernails and toenails should be trimmed.
- Eyeglasses should be secured to prevent slipping.

Gymnasts often use personal equipment, such as hand grips and gymnastics shoes, during gymnastics activities. Coaches and athletes should inspect these items regularly for proper fit as well as wear and tear.

...ING TIP At the start of a season or session, communicate your **...es regarding proper practice and competition attire, as well as other rules and expectations, to athletes and their parents. This can be done via a team handbook or during a parent meeting. Educate all of the participants early, and then consistently enforce the rules throughout the season.**

Coaches should also be aware of their own attire from both a professional and safety perspective. Check with your gymnastics club, which will likely have a dress code for all staff. In general, coaches' attire should meet the following guidelines:

- A staff shirt, such as a polo-style shirt, T-shirt, or sweatshirt, is best.
- Wear athletic-style pants or shorts (appropriate length).
- Athletic shoes with rubberized soles are the best shoes for coaching.
- If you have long hair, secure it away from the face.
- Avoid jeans, baggy clothing, zippers, ties, and other adornments on clothing.
- Avoid wearing jewelry, especially dangling earrings, necklaces, watches, bracelets, and rings. They can easily catch on a gymnast while you are spotting or on a piece of equipment.

Meet Entries

At the local level, meets are generally hosted by a gymnastics club, either at its gymnastics center or at an outside venue. A representative from the club is assigned as the meet director and must sanction the meet through the governing body of USA Gymnastics. One of the stipulations of sanctioning a meet with USA Gymnastics is agreeing to abide by the USA Gymnastics *Rules and Policies* and the Junior Olympic competition manuals. Some variance in available apparatus and equipment, competition format, entry fees, awards, and so on is allowed for sanctioned competitions and should be stated in the meet entry materials. Coaches should carefully review the meet entry materials and be sure to submit competition entries by the deadline. *Note:* All coaches and gymnasts participating in USA Gymnastics–sanctioned events must have a valid membership.

COACHING TIP Coaches should carefully monitor their gymnasts' proficiency and competition scores to be sure they are competing at the appropriate level for their ability and are on track for qualifying for the next stage (e.g., from local competition to sectionals, state championships, regional championships, and national championships) or level (e.g., from level 4 to 5 and so on) of competition.

The state and regional administrative committees within USA Gymnastics have the authority to set the meet calendars for the season. These committees are also integral in running state championships and regional championships, respectively.

Rules of Competition

Gymnastics rules are designed to create a safe environment for participants, to allow competitions to run smoothly, and to prevent individuals and clubs from gaining an unfair advantage. Throw out the rules, and a gymnastics meet can quickly turn chaotic and perhaps unsafe. Following is an overview of some of the basic rules in the USA Gymnastics Junior Olympic Program.

Competition Warm-Ups

At a meet, the first order of business is the warm-up. Most competitions start with a general or open warm-up period of 15 to 30 minutes. This is when the gymnasts should go through their typical warm-up routine, including locomotor and aerobic exercises (e.g., running), stretching, and basic skill rehearsals (those that can be done in a confined space). During this time, the apparatus are not available for practicing skills, but gymnasts may check settings.

Next is the timed warm-up period. This is when the gymnasts are able to warm up their competitive skills on the apparatus. Depending on the competition format, the gymnasts may warm up on all events and then compete, or they may warm up on one event and then compete on that event and so forth for the remaining events. As a coach, you should have advance knowledge of the competition format and prepare your athletes accordingly. The gymnasts will be grouped into squads, and there will be a designated amount of time for warm-up on each event. Help your gymnasts use this time wisely, and be considerate of the other gymnasts in the group.

COACHING TIP In practice, try to create a competition-like atmosphere. Try tactics such as timing the gymnasts' warm-up period and length of routines; practicing the events in the order athletes will compete; judging their routines; inviting their parents into the gym to watch the practice session; and practicing a march-in, how to rotate to an event, and saluting to the judges before and after a routine. This can help your gymnasts prepare mentally and feel more confident and comfortable going into a competition.

Again, depending on the competition format, gymnasts may be allowed a 30-second touch warm-up on the apparatus immediately before they compete. Gymnasts should use this time to do a last-minute warm-up so that they feel comfortable with the apparatus and prepared to compete. After the 30-second touch warm-up, competition will begin on that event.

...tion Procedures

more than 20 minutes is allowed between the end of the timed warm-up period and the start of competition. Gymnasts should quickly change, if need be, from their warm-up attire into their competition leotards and warm-up suits. Usually a march-in is done at the beginning of the competition to introduce all of the competitors, teams, coaches, and officials. Additionally, between each competitive event, gymnasts are expected to march with their assigned squad to the next event and present to the chief judge. This involves the gymnasts' lining up in front of the chief judge to show him or her that they are ready for competition on that particular event.

Coaches should receive an order of competition for the meet. This is normally distributed by the meet director in your meet packet at the beginning of the event. Work with your gymnasts to be sure they know when they compete and that they are prepared for their turn.

Before starting her competitive exercise, the gymnast will be signaled by the chief judge. The gymnast must begin immediately after receiving the signal. A gymnast is required to salute the judges both before and after a routine. A salute consists of turning toward the judging panel and raising one arm (figure 3.1) or two arms (figure 3.2). The gymnast then proceeds with the required routine within the time restrictions and, following the completion of the routine, again salutes the judges to signify the end of the routine.

FIGURE 3.1 One-arm salute.   **FIGURE 3.2** Two-arm salute.

Etiquette on the Field of Play

The field of play is made up of the designated areas in the gymnastics center or venue where the training, warm-ups, and competition take place (also known as the competition area). For the safety of all participants, only competing gymnasts and their coaches are allowed within the field of play. Meet officials, including the meet director, meet referee, judges, medical staff, and volunteers involved in conducting the competition, are also allowed within the field of play. Parents and other family members, children of coaches, and spectators should remain in the designated seating area.

Gymnastics No-Nos

It's inevitable that your gymnasts will violate minor rules during practices and meets. But you must make it clear to your gymnasts that some actions are unacceptable and can result in their removal from the practice, the meet, or even the team, depending on the severity of the infraction. Here are some examples from the USA Gymnastics Code of Ethics:

- Engaging in behavior that is so disorderly or inappropriate as to interfere with the orderly conduct of the activity or other members' participation in, or enjoyment of, the activity (which may include unsportsmanlike actions such as swearing, taunting an opponent, or arguing with an official)

- Engaging in conduct that is unfair, including, in particular, attempting to injure, disable, or intentionally interfere with the preparation of a competitor

- Failing to resort in the first instance to the established procedures for challenging a competitive result, contesting a team selection decision, complaining about the conduct of another member, or attempting to reverse a policy adopted by USA Gymnastics

Your role as a coach is not limited to teaching fundamentals; you must also promote good sporting behavior both in and out of the gym. For example, encourage your gymnasts to wish other competitors well before a competition, to help the coaches straighten up the equipment after practice, and to offer support to teammates who are struggling to learn a complex new skill. Everyone involved with the team will appreciate this behavior.

It is also important to teach your gymnasts how to win and lose with grace. They should exhibit sportsmanship at all times, but especially at the conclusion of a competition. A gesture such as shaking a competitor's hand on the awards podium sends a positive message to all participants. Coaches can model this type of positive behavior by congratulating other coaches, thanking the judges and other meet officials, and praising their gymnast's performance.

Competitors, coaches, and others on the field of play should remember to set cell phones to the off or vibrate position so as to not cause a disruption during competition. If a call must be made, the person should leave the field of play to do this. Gymnasts and coaches should keep their personal equipment, such as gym bags, clothing, and grips, in designated areas out of the way of other competitors.

As a coach, you should understand the rules of competition and have a good grasp of judging rules and deductions. In most cases, a penalty (taken from the gymnast's score) occurs if a coach or another teammate attempts to coach or assist the competing gymnast with verbal cues during a routine. Cheers such as "Come on," "Let's go," and "You can do it" are fine, but be careful about providing coaching advice. Additional deductions can be taken for spotting during a competitive routine, standing on or near the competitive apparatus, not spotting when required, or not obeying apparatus-related rules.

Audience Etiquette

It is important for coaches to educate parents and other spectators about competition etiquette and expectations. Help them understand the flow of the meet, scoring, professional responsibilities, and regulations for their own behavior. Standard regulations typically include the following:

- Remain in the designated area for the public.
- Do not use flash photography during premeet warm-ups or competition.
- Do not disturb the order of the meet, its competitors, or officials.
- Be respectful to all competitors, coaches, and judges.

Your team may have other expectations and responsibilities for parents, so be sure to communicate those as well.

Officials

Gymnastics officials are present at meets to enforce the rules of competition and score the competitive exercises. The scope and level of the particular competition will determine the number of officials and specific assignments. Competition officials may include the following people:

Meet Director Is responsible for the overall planning, organization, and running of the competition. At the Junior Olympic level, especially for local and invitational meets, the meet director might be a parent or other volunteer. However, the meet director must be a professional member of USA Gymnastics.

Meet Referee Works to ensure a smooth-running event from the judging and technical perspective. Meet referees are contracted through the meet director and the designated contractor or assignor.

Judges   Also contracted through the meet director and designated contractor or assignor. Certification, experience, and affiliation are considerations when assigning judges. Depending on the level of competition, one- or two-judge panels are required for each event. A panel typically consists of a chief judge and a panel judge, though some events may utilize a four-judge panel.

Scorer   Records the judges' scores and assists with reports and score flashing.

Timer   Times the length of exercises and falls.

Line Judge   Watches for out-of-bounds violations on the floor exercise.

Flasher   Flashes or posts gymnasts' scores for the competitors and audience to see during the event.

Runner   Runs the judges' score slips from the judges to the scorers and flashers.

Announcer   Introduces competitors and award winners and makes announcements throughout the event.

Music Assistant   Plays floor exercise music (in women's artistic gymnastics) for each competitor.

Awards Presenter   Organizes awards, prints labels, and helps distribute the awards to winners.

Medical Staff   An important part of any athletic event. Can provide emergency and nonemergency care in the case of injuries.

Scoring

An exercise is evaluated based on successful completion of required elements; performance of bonus elements; the execution, artistry, and composition of elements performed; and the impression of the overall exercise. In general, exercises in the Junior Olympic Program start from a 10.0 (for women) and 16.0 (for men), and judges subtract performance errors from that value to arrive at the exercise score.

Each judge on a panel determines a score for the exercise. If a two-judge panel is used, the judges' scores are averaged together. From this average, the chief judge may take additional deductions (neutral deductions) for penalties such as exceeding time allowances, going out of bounds, not presenting to the judges, receiving coaching assistance, wearing incorrect attire, and using mats without authorization to determine the final score. Typically, only this final score is flashed to the competitors and the audience.

If a coach believes there is an error in the score, she is entitled to view the individual judges' scores and neutral deductions. A complete inquiry process is defined in the USA Gymnastics *Rules and Policies* manual. If a dispute over score arises, it is the coach's responsibility to follow the inquiry process. It is unprofessional and sets a poor example for the athletes if you verbally confront a judge or other competition official regarding a disagreement.

Providing for Gymnasts' Safety

4

SAFETY

Safety first! The primary goal of any gymnastics coach is to provide a safe environment for the participants. And the most important factor in safety awareness is the training and education of gymnastics coaches and instructors. A safety mind-set should be incorporated into all program policies and practices.

No coach wants to see athletes get hurt. But injury remains a reality of sport participation; consequently, you must be prepared to provide first aid when injuries occur and to protect yourself against unjustified lawsuits. Fortunately, coaches can institute many preventive measures to reduce such risks. In this chapter, we describe steps you can take to prevent injuries, first aid and emergency responses for when injuries occur, and your legal responsibilities as a coach.

Game Plan for Safety

You can't prevent all injuries from happening, but you can take preventive measures that give your gymnasts the best possible chance for injury-free participation. To help you create the safest possible environment for your athletes, we'll explore what you can do in these areas:

- Preseason physical examinations
- Physical conditioning
- Facilities and equipment inspection
- Inherent risks
- Proper supervision and record keeping
- Environmental conditions

Preseason Physical Examinations

We recommend that your athletes have a physical examination before participating in gymnastics. The exam should address the most likely areas of medical concern and identify youngsters at high risk. We also suggest that you ask gymnasts' parents or guardians to sign a participation agreement form (discussed in more detail later in this chapter) and an informed consent form to allow their children to be treated in case of an emergency (see "Sample Consent to Treatment Form" on page 251 of the appendix).

Physical Conditioning

Gymnasts need to be in shape (or get in shape) to participate at the level expected. They must have adequate cardiorespiratory fitness and muscular fitness.

Cardiorespiratory fitness involves the body's ability to use oxygen and fuels efficiently to power muscle contractions. As athletes get in better shape, their bodies are able to more efficiently deliver oxygen to fuel muscles and carry off carbon dioxide and other wastes. At times, gymnastics will require a great deal of exertion. Youngsters who aren't as fit as their peers often overextend in trying to keep up, which can result in light-headedness, nausea, fatigue, and injury.

Try to remember that the kids' goals are to participate, learn, and have fun. Therefore, you must keep your gymnasts active, attentive, and involved with every phase of practice. If you do, they will attain higher levels of cardiorespiratory fitness as the season progresses simply by taking part in practice. However, you should watch closely for signs of low cardiorespiratory fitness; don't let your gymnasts overdo it as they build their fitness. You might privately counsel youngsters who appear overly winded, suggesting that they train outside of practice (under proper supervision) to increase their fitness.

Muscular fitness encompasses strength, muscular endurance, power, speed, and flexibility. This type of fitness is affected by physical maturity as well as various types of training. Your gymnasts will likely exhibit a relatively wide range of muscular fitness. Gymnasts who are fit will sustain fewer muscular injuries, and any injuries that do occur will tend to be minor. And in case of injury, recovery is faster in athletes with higher levels of muscular fitness.

COACHING TIP Younger athletes may not be aware of when they need a break for water and a short rest; therefore, you need to work breaks into your practice schedules. In addition, you should have water available at all times during the practice session. The athletes will have different hydration needs, and making water accessible will allow them to grab a drink when they need it and will reduce the need for long water breaks during the practice session.

Two other components of fitness and injury prevention are the warm-up and the cool-down. Although young bodies are generally very limber, they can become tight through inactivity. The warm-up should address each muscle group and should elevate the heart rate in preparation for strenuous activity. Gymnasts should warm up for 5 to 10 minutes using a combination of light running, skipping, easy jumping, and loosening moves. As practice winds down, slow their heart rates with an easy jog or walk. Then have them stretch for 5 minutes to help prevent tight muscles before the next practice or competition.

Facilities and Equipment Inspection

Another way to prevent injuries is to regularly examine the equipment and apparatus on which your gymnasts practice. Remove hazards, report conditions you cannot remedy, and request maintenance as necessary. If unsafe conditions exist, you should either make adaptations to prevent risk to your athletes' safety or stop the practice or competition until safe conditions have been restored. You can also prevent injuries by checking the quality and fit of uniforms, practice attire, and any protective equipment used by your gymnasts. Refer to "Sample Facility Inspection Form" in the appendix (page 241) to guide you in verifying that facilities and equipment are safe.

To prepare a safe environment, you should do the following:

- Be in the gym well before class starts.
- Set up stations and activities before class. Set out all needed props and other equipment that may be in storage.
- Do a final walk-through to ensure that all equipment is placed safely.
- Ensure that a coach who is properly trained and prepared to meet the needs of the gymnasts is present.
- Review proper instructions for the use of equipment, apparatus, and props.
- Educate the gymnasts regarding safety rules as well as proper landing and falling techniques (see page 93 of chapter 7).

Inherent Risks

As a gymnastics coach, you must warn athletes of the inherent risks involved in participating in gymnastics, because "failure to warn" is one of the most successful arguments in lawsuits against coaches. So, thoroughly explain the inherent risks of gymnastics, and make sure each gymnast knows, understands, and appreciates those risks. You can learn more about inherent risks by referring to USA Gymnastics' *Gymnastics Risk Management*.

The preseason parent orientation meeting is a good opportunity to explain the risks of the sport to both parents and gymnasts. It is also a good time to have both the gymnasts and their parents sign a participation agreement form or waiver releasing you from liability should an injury occur (see "Sample Registration Form With Waiver and Release" on page 247 of the appendix). You should consult with an attorney in your area who is familiar with the sport and with local ordinances when creating these forms or waivers. These forms or waivers do not relieve you of responsibility for your gymnasts' well-being, but they are recommended by lawyers and are a necessary practice for gymnastics coaches and businesses.

Proper Supervision and Record Keeping

To ensure athletes' safety, you must provide both indirect and direct supervision. *Indirect supervision* means you are in the area of activity so you can see and hear what is happening. You should be

- at the gymnastics facility and in position to supervise the gymnasts even before the formal practice begins,
- immediately accessible to the activity and able to oversee the entire activity,
- alert to conditions that may be dangerous to the gymnasts and ready to take action to protect the gymnasts,

- able to react immediately and appropriately to emergencies, and
- present at the gymnastics facility until the last gymnast has been picked up after the practice or competition.

Direct supervision involves actively overseeing an activity during practice. For example, you should provide direct supervision when you teach a new skill and should continue it until your gymnasts understand the requirements of the skill, the risks involved, and their own ability to perform in light of these risks. You must also provide direct supervision when you notice athletes breaking rules or notice a change in the condition of your athletes. As a general rule, the more dangerous the activity, the more direct the supervision required. This suggests that more direct supervision is required with younger and less experienced gymnasts as well as for older gymnasts who are learning and practicing more dangerous skills.

COACHING TIP Common sense tells us that it's easier to provide direct supervision to a smaller group of athletes, regardless of age. Enlist the help of assistant coaches so that you can divide your team into smaller groups. This will help ensure that your gymnasts can practice skills in a safe environment. The more adults who can help supervise, the better the gymnasts can learn and perform the necessary skills. In addition, smaller groups allow each coach to provide more direct feedback to athletes.

As part of your supervisory duty, you are expected to foresee potentially dangerous situations and to be positioned to help prevent them. This requires that you know gymnastics well, especially the rules that are intended to provide for safety. Prohibit dangerous horseplay, and hold training sessions only under safe conditions. These direct supervisory activities, performed consistently, will make the environment safer for your gymnasts and will help protect you from liability if a mishap occurs.

For further protection, keep records of your season plans, practice plans, and athletes' injuries. Season and practice plans come in handy when you need evidence that gymnasts have been taught certain skills, while accurate and detailed injury report forms offer protection against unfounded lawsuits. Ask for these forms from your sponsoring organization (see "Sample Incident Report Form" on page 250 in the appendix), and hold onto these records for several years so that an old injury doesn't come back to haunt you.

Environmental Conditions

Although gymnastics is an indoor sport, coaches must still be aware of environmental conditions that may affect their athletes. Most health problems caused by environmental factors are related to excessive heat or cold. A little thought about the

potential problems and a little effort to ensure adequate protection for your gymnasts will prevent most serious emergencies related to environmental conditions.

> **COACHING TIP** Encourage your gymnasts to drink plenty of water before, during, and after practice. Water makes up 45 to 65 percent of a youngster's body weight, and even a small amount of water loss can cause severe damage to the body's systems. It doesn't have to be hot and humid for athletes to become dehydrated, nor is thirst an accurate indicator. In fact, by the time athletes are aware of their thirst, they are long overdue for a drink.

Heat

On hot, humid days the body has difficulty cooling itself. Because the air is already saturated with water vapor (humidity), sweat doesn't evaporate as easily. Therefore, body sweat is a less effective cooling agent, and the body retains extra heat. Hot, humid environments put athletes at risk of heat exhaustion and heatstroke (see more on these in "Serious Injuries" on pages 44 and 45). And if *you* think it's hot or humid, it's worse for the kids, not only because they're more active but also because kids under the age of 12 have more difficulty regulating their body temperature than adults do. To provide for your gymnasts' safety in hot or humid conditions, take the following preventive measures:

- Monitor conditions within the practice facility, and adjust practices accordingly. Although many gyms are air-conditioned, "hot spots" may still exist.
- Adjust clothing if necessary (e.g., remove warm-ups).
- Identify and monitor athletes who are prone to heat illness. This would include gymnasts who are overweight, heavily muscled, or out of shape and gymnasts who work excessively hard or have previously suffered from heat illness. Closely monitor these athletes, and give them frequent fluid breaks.
- Make sure athletes replace fluids lost through sweat. Fluids such as water and sports drinks are preferable during competitions and practices.
- Encourage athletes to replenish electrolytes, such as sodium (salt) and potassium, that are lost through sweat. The best way to replace these nutrients—as well as others such as carbohydrate (for energy) and protein (for muscle building)—is by eating a balanced diet.

Cold

When a person is exposed to cold weather, body temperature starts to drop below normal. To counteract this reaction, the body shivers to create heat and reduces blood flow to the extremities to conserve heat in the core of the body. To reduce the risk of cold-related injuries, make certain that the temperature of your practice facility is appropriate for outdoor conditions and that your gymnasts warm up thoroughly. Keep gymnasts active to maintain body heat, and make sure they wear appropriate protective clothing when coming in from and going out into the cold.

Responding to Athletes' Injuries

No matter how thorough your prevention program is, injuries most likely will occur. When injury does strike, chances are that you will be the one in charge. The severity and nature of the injury will determine how actively involved you'll be in treating it. But regardless of how seriously an athlete is hurt, it is your responsibility to know what steps to take. Therefore, you must be prepared to take appropriate action and provide basic emergency care when an injury occurs.

Being Prepared

Being prepared to provide basic emergency care involves many things, including being trained in cardiopulmonary resuscitation (CPR) and first aid and having an emergency action plan.

CPR and First Aid Training

We recommend that all coaches receive CPR and first aid training from a nationally recognized organization such as the National Safety Council, the American Heart Association, the American Red Cross, USA Gymnastics, or the American Sport Education Program (ASEP). Canadian organizations that offer training are the Heart and Stroke Foundation of Canada and the Canadian Red Cross. You should be certified based on a practical test and a written test of knowledge. CPR training should include pediatric and adult basic life support and procedures for dealing with an obstructed airway. *Note:* USA Gymnastics has an online first aid course specifically written for gymnastics.

Emergency Plan

An emergency plan is the final step in being prepared to take appropriate action for serious injuries. The plan calls for three steps:

1. **Evaluate the injured athlete.**

Use your CPR and first aid training to guide you. Be sure to keep these certifications up to date. Practice your skills frequently to keep them fresh and ready to use if and when you need them.

2. **Call the appropriate medical personnel.**

If possible, delegate the responsibility of seeking medical help to another calm and responsible adult who attends all practices and competitions. Write out a list of emergency phone numbers, and keep it with you at practices and competitions. Include the following phone numbers:

- Rescue unit
- Hospital
- Physician

- Police
- Fire department

Take each gymnast's emergency information to every practice and competition (see "Emergency Information Card" on page 252 of the appendix). This information includes the person to contact in case of an emergency, what types of medications the athlete is using, what types of drugs the athlete is allergic to, and so on.

Give an "Emergency Response Card" (see page 253 of the appendix) to the contact person calling for emergency assistance. Having this information ready should help the contact person remain calm. You must also complete an incident report form (see a sample form on page 250 of the appendix); keep one on file for every injury that occurs.

First Aid Kit

A well-stocked first aid kit should include the following:

- Antibacterial soap or wipes
- Arm sling
- Athletic tape—1.5 inches (3.8 cm)
- Bandage scissors
- Bandage strips—assorted sizes
- Blood spill kit
- Cell phone
- Contact lens case
- Cotton swabs
- Elastic wraps—3 inches (8 cm), 4 inches (10 cm), and 6 inches (15 cm)
- Emergency blanket
- Examination gloves (latex free)
- Eye patch
- Foam rubber—1/8 inch (.3 cm), 1/4 inch (.6 cm), and 1/2 inch (1.2 cm)
- Insect sting kit
- List of emergency phone numbers
- Mirror

- Moleskin
- Nail clippers
- Oral thermometer (to determine if a gymnast has a fever caused by illness)
- Penlight
- Petroleum jelly
- Plastic bags (for crushed ice)
- Prewrap (underwrap for tape)
- Rescue breathing or CPR face mask
- Safety glasses (for assistance in first aid)
- Safety pins
- Saline solution (for eyes)
- Sterile gauze pads—3-inch (8 cm) and 4-inch (10 cm) squares (preferably nonstick)
- Sterile gauze rolls
- Tape adherent and tape remover
- Tongue depressors
- Tooth saver kit
- Triangular bandages
- Tweezers

SAFETY

Adapted, by permission, from M. Flegel, 2008, *Sport first aid*, 4th ed. (Champaign, IL: Human Kinetics), 20.

Emergency Steps

You must have a clear, well-rehearsed emergency action plan. You want to be sure you are prepared in case of an emergency because every second counts. Your emergency plan should follow this sequence:

1. Check the athlete's level of consciousness.
2. Send a contact person to call the appropriate medical personnel and to locate or call the gymnast's parents.
3. Send someone to wait for the rescue team and direct them to the injured athlete.
4. Assess the injury.
5. Administer first aid.
6. Assist emergency medical personnel in preparing the athlete for transportation to a medical facility.
7. Appoint someone to go with the athlete if the parents are not available. This person should be responsible, calm, and familiar with the athlete. Assistant coaches or other parents are best for this job.
8. Complete an incident report form while the incident is fresh in your mind (see page 250 of the appendix).

3. Provide first aid.

If medical personnel are not on hand at the time of the injury, you should provide first aid care to the extent of your qualifications. Again, although your CPR and first aid training will guide you, you must remember the following:

- Do not move the injured athlete if the injury is to the head, neck, or back; if a large joint (ankle, knee, elbow, or shoulder) is dislocated; or if the pelvis, a rib, or an arm or leg is fractured.
- Calm the injured athlete, and keep others away from him as much as possible.
- Evaluate whether the athlete's breathing has stopped or is irregular, and if necessary, clear the airway with your fingers.
- Administer CPR as directed in the CPR certification course recommended by your school, league, or state association.
- Remain with the athlete until medical personnel arrive.

Taking Appropriate Action

Proper CPR and first aid training, a well-stocked first aid kit, and an emergency plan help prepare you to take appropriate action when an injury occurs. In the previous section, we mention the importance of providing first aid to the extent of your qualifications. Don't "play doctor" with injuries; sort out minor injuries that you can treat from those that need medical attention. Now let's look at the appropriate action for minor injuries and more serious injuries.

Minor Injuries

Although no injury seems minor to the person experiencing it, most injuries are neither life threatening nor severe enough to restrict participation. When these injuries occur, you can take an active role in their initial treatment.

Scrapes and Cuts   When one of your gymnasts has an open wound, the first thing you should do is put on a pair of disposable latex-free examination gloves or some other effective blood barrier. Then follow these four steps:

1. Stop the bleeding by applying direct pressure with a clean dressing to the wound and elevating it. The gymnast may be able to apply this pressure while you put on your gloves. Do not remove the dressing if it becomes soaked with blood. Instead, place an additional dressing on top of the one already in place. If bleeding does not stop, continue to elevate the injured area above the heart and maintain pressure.

2. Cleanse the wound thoroughly once the bleeding is controlled. A good rinsing with a forceful stream of water, and perhaps light scrubbing with soap, will help prevent infection.

3. Protect the wound with sterile gauze or a bandage strip. If the gymnast continues to participate, apply protective padding over the injured area.

4. Remove and dispose of gloves carefully to keep yourself (or anyone else) from coming into contact with blood.

COACHING TIP   You shouldn't let a fear of acquired immune deficiency syndrome (AIDS) and other communicable diseases stop you from helping an athlete. You are at risk only if you allow contaminated blood to come in contact with an open wound on your body, so the examination gloves that you wear will protect you from AIDS if one of your athletes carries this disease. Check with your sport director, your league, or the Centers for Disease Control and Prevention (CDC) for more information about protecting yourself and your participants from AIDS.

For bloody noses not associated with serious facial injury, have the gymnast sit and lean slightly forward. Then pinch the gymnast's nostrils shut. If the bleeding continues for several minutes, or if the gymnast has a history of nosebleeds, seek medical assistance.

Strains and Sprains The physical demands of participating in gymnastics often result in injury to the muscles or tendons (strains) or to the ligaments (sprains). When your gymnasts suffer minor strains or sprains, you should immediately apply the PRICE method of injury care:

P Protect the athlete and the injured body part from further danger or trauma.

R Rest the injured area to avoid further damage and to foster healing.

I Ice the area to reduce swelling and pain.

C Compress the area by securing an ice bag in place with an elastic wrap.

E Elevate the injury above heart level to keep the blood from pooling in the area.

Bumps and Bruises Inevitably, gymnasts make contact with one another, with an apparatus, and with the floor. If the force applied to a body part at impact is great enough, a bump or bruise will result. Many athletes continue to participate with such sore spots, but if the bump or bruise is large and painful, you should take appropriate action. Again, use the PRICE method for injury care, and monitor the injury. If swelling, discoloration, and pain have lessened, the gymnast may resume participation with protective padding; if not, the gymnast should be examined by a physician.

Serious Injuries

Head, neck, and back injuries; fractures; and injuries that cause an athlete to lose consciousness are among a class of injuries that you cannot and should not try to treat yourself. In these cases, you should follow the emergency plan outlined on page 37.

If you suspect that a gymnast has received a blow to the head, no matter how mild the symptoms, you should view it as a serious injury. If the gymnast has only mild symptoms, such as a headache, call the parents and have them take the gymnast to a doctor immediately. You should alert emergency medical services (EMS) immediately if the gymnast has lost consciousness or has impaired memory, dizziness, ringing in the ears, blood or fluid draining from the nose or ears, or blurry vision. For more information, see the "Heads Up: Concussion in Youth Sports" fact sheet, provided by the Centers for Disease Control and Prevention (www.cdc.gov), on page 42. If you suspect that a gymnast has a spine injury, joint dislocation, or bone fracture, do not move the gymnast unless you have to do so to provide lifesaving CPR.

Heads Up: Concussion in Youth Sports

What Is a Concussion?

A concussion is a brain injury. Concussions are caused by a bump or blow to the head. Even a "ding," "getting your bell rung," or what seems to be a mild bump or blow to the head can be serious.

You can't see a concussion. Signs and symptoms of concussion can show up right after the injury or may not appear or be noticed until days or weeks after the injury. If your child reports any symptoms of concussion, or if you notice the symptoms yourself, seek medical attention right away.

What Are the Signs and Symptoms of a Concussion?

SIGNS OBSERVED BY PARENTS OR GUARDIANS

If a child has experienced a bump or blow to the head during a competition or practice, look for any of the following signs and symptoms of a concussion:

- Appears dazed or stunned
- Is confused
- Forgets an instruction
- Moves clumsily
- Answers questions slowly
- Loses consciousness (even briefly)
- Shows behavior or personality changes
- Can't recall events before hit or fall
- Can't recall events after hit or fall

SYMPTOMS REPORTED BY ATHLETE

- Headache or pressure in head
- Nausea or vomiting
- Balance problems or dizziness
- Double or blurry vision
- Sensitivity to light
- Sensitivity to noise
- Feeling sluggish, hazy, foggy, or groggy
- Concentration or memory problems
- Confusion
- Does not "feel right"

How Can You Help Children Prevent a Concussion?

Every sport is different, but there are steps children can take to protect themselves from concussion.

- Ensure that they follow their coach's rules for safety and the rules of the sport.
- Encourage them to practice good sportsmanship at all times.
- Learn the signs and symptoms of a concussion.

What Should You Do if You Think a Child Has a Concussion?

1. **Seek medical attention right away.** A health care professional will be able to decide how serious the concussion is and when it is safe for the child to return to sports.

2. **Keep the child out of play.** Concussions take time to heal. Don't let the child return to play until a health care professional says it's OK. Athletes who return to play too soon—while the brain is still healing—risk a greater chance of having a second concussion. Second or later concussions can be very serious. They can cause permanent brain damage, affecting the child for a lifetime.

3. **Tell other coaches about any recent concussion.** All coaches and staff at the club should know if a child has had a recent concussion in *any* sport. Other staff at your club might not know about a concussion the child has suffered in another sport or activity unless you tell them.

Adapted from Centers for Disease Control and Prevention, 2007, Heads up: Concussion in youth sports: A fact sheet for parents. [Online]. Available: http://www.cdc.gov/concussion/pdf/parents_Eng.pdf [August 18, 2010].

We do want to examine more closely, however, your role in preventing and attending to heat cramps, heat exhaustion, and heatstroke. Additionally, refer to figure 4.1 on page 44 for an illustrative example of the signs and symptoms associated with heat exhaustion and heatstroke.

Heat Cramps Tough practices combined with heat stress and substantial fluid loss from sweating can provoke muscle cramps commonly known as *heat cramps.* Cramping is most common when the weather is hot. Depending on your location, it may be hot early in the season, which can be problematic because athletes may be less conditioned and less adapted to heat. In other locations, it may be hot later in the season, when athletes are better conditioned but still not used to participating in high temperatures. A cramp, a severe tightening of

Heat exhaustion

- Headache
- Dizziness
- Fatigue
- Dehydration
- Profuse sweating
- Mildly increased body temperature
- Nausea or vomiting
- Diarrhea
- Muscle cramps

Heatstroke

- Headache
- Dizziness
- Disoriented, combative, or unconscious
- Dehydration
- Severely increased body temperature
- Hot and wet or dry skin
- Nausea or vomiting
- Diarrhea

FIGURE 4.1 Signs and symptoms of heat exhaustion and heatstroke.

the muscle, can drop athletes and prevent continued participation. Dehydration, electrolyte loss, and fatigue are the contributing factors. The immediate treatment is to have the gymnast cool off, replace fluids lost through activity, and slowly stretch the contracted muscle. The gymnast may resume participation later that same day or the next day provided the cramp doesn't cause a muscle strain.

Heat Exhaustion Heat exhaustion is a shocklike condition caused by strenuous activity combined with heat stress. This, in addition to dehydration and electrolyte depletion, does not allow the body to keep up. Symptoms include fatigue, dizziness, headache, nausea, vomiting, diarrhea, and muscle cramps. Difficulty continuing the activity, profuse sweating, and mildly increased body temperature are key signs of heat exhaustion.

A gymnast suffering from heat exhaustion should rest in a cool area with her legs propped above heart level; remove excess clothing and equipment; drink cool fluids, particularly those containing electrolytes (if not nauseated); and apply ice to the neck, back, or abdomen to help cool the body. If you believe that a gymnast is suffering from heat exhaustion, seek medical attention. Under no conditions should the gymnast return to activity that day. In this situation, we recommend that the gymnast not return to activity until she has a written release from a physician.

Heatstroke Heatstroke is a life-threatening condition in which the body stops sweating and body temperature rises dangerously high. It results from the continuation of strenuous activity in extreme temperatures. Heatstroke occurs when dehydration and electrolyte depletion cause a malfunction in the body's temperature control center in the brain. Symptoms include fatigue, dizziness, confusion, irritability, hysteria, nausea, vomiting, diarrhea, and the feeling of being extremely hot. Signs include hot and wet or dry skin; rapid pulse and rapid breathing; and possible seizures, unconsciousness, or respiratory or cardiac arrest.

If you suspect that an athlete is suffering from heatstroke, send for emergency medical assistance immediately, and cool the athlete as quickly as possible. Remove excess clothing and cool the athlete's body with cool, wet towels; by pouring cool water over the athlete; or by placing the athlete in a cold bath. Apply ice packs to the armpits, neck, back, abdomen, and between the legs. If the athlete is conscious, give him cool fluids to drink. If the athlete is unconscious or falls unconscious, place him on his side to allow fluids and vomit to drain from the mouth. A gymnast who has suffered heatstroke may not return to the gym until he has a written release from a physician.

Protecting Yourself

When one of your gymnasts is injured, naturally your first concern is the athlete's well-being. Your desire to help youngsters, after all, was what made you decide to coach. Unfortunately, you must also consider something else: Can you be held liable for the injury?

From a legal standpoint, a coach must fulfill eight duties. We've discussed all but planning in this chapter (planning is discussed in chapters 5 and 13. The following is a summary of your legal duties:

1. Provide a safe environment.
2. Properly plan the activity.
3. Provide adequate and proper equipment.
4. Warn of inherent risks in the sport.
5. Supervise the activity closely.
6. Evaluate athletes for injury or incapacitation.
7. Know emergency procedures, CPR, and first aid.
8. Keep adequate records.

In addition to fulfilling these eight legal duties, you should check your organization's insurance coverage and your own personal insurance coverage to make sure these policies will properly protect you from liability.

USA Gymnastics offers safety and risk management certification courses online and face to face throughout the United States. For more information about the courses or to register, visit www.usagym.org.

Making Practices Fun and Effective

5

Before you begin, consider why your athletes decided to become involved with gymnastics. Children choose to play sports for many reasons, but two of the most common are to have fun and develop skills. So that's exactly what your goal should be while teaching your athletes. This chapter will provide advice on how to maximize the learning environment for your gymnasts while also allowing them to have an enjoyable experience.

In addition to planning for the entire season, it is important to plan for each practice. The more organized the class, the better the gymnasts learn. What you plan for each class must be reasonable for the skill level and maturity of the gymnasts. Teach novice gymnasts the basic body positions and movements. Move on to specific progressions for more difficult skills only after the gymnasts have mastered these basics.

Planning the Lesson

Lesson planning includes identifying the specific skills you will teach your gymnasts; developing lead-ups, progressions, and drills related to those skills; and then organizing them into the various practice sessions. As important as it is to have a lesson plan, it is also important to be flexible. If your gymnasts are having a difficult time learning a particular skill, take some extra time to practice the skill—even if that means moving back your overall schedule. After all, if your gymnasts cannot perform the fundamental skills, they will not be able to execute the more difficult skills properly or safely.

Select skills for each lesson that will incorporate tasks in all three developmental domains: psychomotor (physical), affective (social and emotional), and cognitive (mental). See figure 5.1. Often, coaches focus solely on the physical benefits of sport, but young athletes are at a critical stage of learning cognitive and affective skills, which they will use for the rest of their lives. Take the opportunity to enhance your gymnasts' skills in each developmental area.

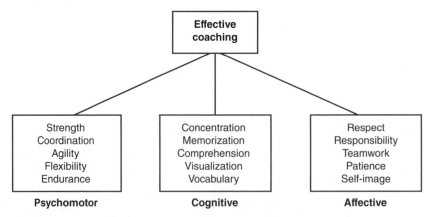

FIGURE 5.1 Effective instruction includes developmental tasks from the psychomotor, cognitive, and affective domains.

Adapted, by permission, from American Sport Education Program, 1992, *Rookie coaches gymnastics guide* (Champaign, IL: Human Kinetics), 54.

COACHING TIP Ways to incorporate affective and cognitive skill development into your lesson plans involve adding new skills and progressions, rotation patterns, or equipment configurations to create unique teaching and learning environments. By adding such new elements, gymnasts can increase their gymnastics vocabulary and feel the achievement of accomplishing a new task.

Lessons should be structured to maximize the gymnasts' on-task time and their success rate. Keep the gymnasts busy during class and they will learn more, have more fun, and likely have fewer behavior problems. It is helpful to establish performance goals for each class and include a variety of activities to help the gymnasts accomplish these goals. As you plan your lessons, keep in mind your gymnasts' learning styles, and vary your teaching methods to optimize learning for all the participants.

Guided Discovery

The guided discovery, or cooperative, method of teaching is often an effective teaching style. It allows kids to discover what to do, not by your telling them but by their experiencing it. It empowers the gymnasts to solve problems that arise by themselves, which is a large part of the fun in learning. Here are four steps to using the guided discovery approach in your classes.

Step 1: Stage a Modified Activity

Modifying the activity or task lets you emphasize a limited number of technical aspects. This is one way to guide your gymnasts to discover certain methods that will improve performance. In gymnastics, we often call a modified activity a lead-up or drill (see page 91 of chapter 7).

For instance, when teaching a back extension roll, you could set up several stations that allow the gymnasts to practice parts of the skill. At one station you may have them practice a backward roll to candlestick position then back to stand. At another station the gymnasts could try a backward roll to a pike stand. And a third station could allow the gymnasts to practice a handstand with a step-down. The goal of these stations is for the gymnasts to feel and understand the required body movements and positions that will transfer to the back extension roll. The drills should be at a level where the gymnasts can safely attempt them without a spotter. This will allow the gymnasts to think about what they need to do in order to perform the skill.

Activities Checklist

When developing activities, or drills, for your youth gymnastics program, here are a few questions you should ask yourself:

- Are the activities fun?
- Are the activities organized?
- Are the gymnasts involved in the activities?
- Do the activities require the gymnasts to use creativity and decision making?
- Are the spaces used appropriate for the activities?
- Is your feedback appropriate?
- Are there implications for other gymnastics skills?

Step 2: Help Athletes Understand the Activity

As your athletes participate in the modified activities, or drills, you should look for the right spot to freeze the action, step in, and ask questions about errors you're seeing. When you do this, you help the athletes better understand the objective of the drill, what they must do to achieve that objective, and also what technique they must use.

Asking the right questions is a very important part of your teaching. Essentially, you'll be asking your athletes—often literally—"What do you need to do to succeed in this situation?" Sometimes athletes simply need to gain more experience, or you may need to modify the task further so that it is even easier for them to discover what they need to do. It may take more patience on your part, but it's a powerful way for athletes to learn. For example, let's say your gymnasts are participating in a drill in which the objective is to hurdle onto a vaulting board and perform a straight jump onto a raised mat. Ask the gymnasts the following questions:

- What are you supposed to do in this activity?
- What do you have to do to jump and land properly on the mat?
- How do you respond after failed attempts?

COACHING TIP If your athletes have trouble understanding what to do, you can phrase your questions to let the athletes choose between two options. For example, if you ask, "What's the best way to correct your hurdle to allow you to rebound off the board?" and an athlete responds, "Circling my arms," then ask, "Do you circle your arms before the hurdle or during the hurdle?"

At first, asking the right questions might seem difficult because your athletes might have little or no experience with the sport. You must resist the powerful temptation to tell your athletes what to do. Instead, through modified activities and skillful questioning on your part, your athletes should come to realize on their own that technical awareness and appropriate fundamentals, intensity, and emotional control are essential for success. Just as important, instead of telling them what the critical skills are, you have led them to this discovery.

Step 3: Teach the Skills of the Activity

Only when your athletes recognize the skills they need in order to be successful do you want to put those parts together into a complete skill or sequence of skills. This is when you use a more traditional approach to teaching sport skills, the IDEA approach, which we describe in chapter 6. This type of teaching breaks down the skills of the events. It should be implemented early in the season so that your gymnasts can begin attaining skills, which will make gymnastics more fun.

Step 4: Practice the Skills in Another Activity

As a coach, you want your athletes to experience success as they're learning skills, and the best way for them to experience this success early on is for you to create an advantage for the athletes. Once the athletes have successfully practiced the drills, as outlined in step 1, you can then have them participate in another activity—this time slightly more challenging (e.g., back roll with straight arms to push-up position) and maybe with aid from a piece of equipment (e.g., back extension roll using an incline mat). Practicing these additional drills will make your gymnasts more likely to reach the goal.

Keep in mind that not all gymnastics skills easily lend themselves to modified activities; such skills may be best taught with individual attention to each gymnast. The key is to set up situations where your athletes experience success yet are challenged in doing so. This will take careful monitoring on your part, but having kids participate in modified activities as they are learning skills is a very effective way of helping them learn and improve.

Activities, Conditioning Ideas, and Games

Here you will find a variety of activities, conditioning ideas, and games that can be used as part of your warm-up or cool-down or may be incorporated into your practice session. These activities address practice organization, conditioning and fitness, motor development, and partner and group experiences.

ACTIVITIES, CONDITIONING IDEAS, AND GAMES

➤ COOKIE MONSTER

Goal Promote cardiorespiratory exercise; good for inclusion in warm-up or group activities.

Description Have the children stand in a straight line against the wall, with one child standing some distance away. The children in line are cookies, and the other child is the cookie monster. The children chant, "Cookie monster, cookie monster, what time is it?" The cookie monster responds with a clock time of her choice. If she chooses eight o'clock, for example, the cookies count together as they take eight large steps toward the cookie monster. The cookies repeat their chant, and the cookie monster continues to respond with times until she decides to answer "Cookie time!" At that time, the cookie monster chases the cookies back to the wall.

Variations

- Change cookie monsters often.
- Instead of walking forward, vary the activity the athletes do to move forward (e.g., lunges, animal movements, skips, or hops).

➤ HOOPERS

Goal Work on locomotion as well as cardiorespiratory fitness and strength.

Description Place half as many hoops on the floor as the number of children. Have the children stand outside the hoops. On the command "Run," the children run around the area without touching each other or the hoops. On the command "Hoopers," each child must try to jump inside the nearest hoop. The children without hoops must perform an exercise, such as push-ups or jumping jacks.

Variations

- Instead of running, vary the actions outside the hoops, such as galloping, turning, jumping, or skipping.
- Vary the exercises done by the children without hoops.
- Have all the children participate in the exercises, instead of just the ones outside the hoops.

➤ FITNESS RACE TRACK

Goal Promote cardiorespiratory exercise and strength; good for inclusion in warm-up or cool-down activities.

Description Use a large, open area that can be made into a 40-foot (12 m) square. Place cones with signs that have a list of 7 to 10 exercises at the corners of the square. These should be basic, such as sit-ups, push-ups, or cartwheels; the exercises chosen can be related to whatever skills you're teaching or working on that day. The gymnasts form groups of two and go to a corner of the square. Make sure the pairs are distributed evenly among the corners. One partner will be the runner, and the other will be the exerciser. When the high-energy music starts (or on your signal), the runner will run around the square while his partner does the first exercise on the list. When the runner gets back to the corner he started from, he does the first exercise on the list, and his partner becomes the runner. The teams continue until each partner has performed all the exercises on the list. The pair that completes the list of exercises first wins the game. Have the students who are finished walk around inside the square until the other teams have finished the activity.

Variation This activity can also be done without winners. Each team must complete all of the exercises. When they are finished, the athletes move on to additional stretching or cool-down activities.

➤ STICK CONTEST

Goals Practice proper landing positions and sticking dismounts.

Description In one or two lines, the gymnasts practice jumping off a 2-foot (24 inch) block and landing in a safe landing position and freezing (i.e., holding this position without taking a step). As long as the gymnast sticks the landing, he can continue in the game, returning to the back of the line.
   Designate another activity (such as stretching) for those who are out.

Variations

- Vary the jumps from the block—straight jump, tuck jump, jump with a half turn, straight jump backward, and so on.
- Jump off different surfaces or from different heights. The jumping surface should be a stable piece of equipment or apparatus.

➤ RELAY RACES

Goal Promote conditioning and fitness development as well as team building.

Description Divide the gymnasts into teams of three to five. Each team forms a straight line at one end of the floor exercise mat. Make sure there is sufficient room between each line.

On your command, the first member of the team performs the requested skill or activity (e.g., cartwheels or round-offs) down to the other end of the floor and then back. After returning to the line, that gymnast tags the next teammate in line, and that team member performs the skill down and back on the mat. Continue until all teammates have completed the skill. The team who is the first to finish the activity wins.

Variations

- Vary the activities. Use locomotor activities, basic skills and tumbling (e.g., rolls or cartwheels), handstand walks, and so on.
- Vary the reward for the winning team, such as reduced conditioning or names added to a jar for a weekly drawing.

Drills and Routines

Following are some drills and routines to help you maximize both your practice time and gymnast participation. Drills and routines help to encourage proper form and better replicate competition settings.

DRILLS AND ROUTINES

➤ LINE DRILLS

Goal Maximize participation and practice time; especially useful for floor exercise training.

Description Gymnasts line up along one end of the floor exercise mat. There should be sufficient room between gymnasts (greater than arm's length). If the number of gymnasts warrants, form short lines along the edge of the floor.

The gymnasts move across the floor, performing the designated activity. Direct the activity and give feedback as the group performs the skill. This is a great way to incorporate locomotor and tumbling skills into every practice session. This drill can also be helpful as a warm-up for intermediate and advanced skills. This time allows gymnasts to practice previously learned skills.

Variation Vary the activities performed during this time. Each trip across the floor can be a different activity. Activities may include locomotor movements, rolls, leaps and jumps, handstands, or basic tumbling.

➤ HIT ROUTINES

Goal Encourage gymnasts to make their first routine of the practice, applying additional pressure to replicate competition setting.

Description Each gymnast must make (successfully complete) seven routines on the given event (this works for any event). If she makes her first routine, she can reduce the number of routines to six.

Therefore, if the gymnast hits her first routine (i.e., successfully completes all the skills), then she would have five more routines to hit for a total of six. If the gymnast has a fall or misses a skill in her first routine, then she would have seven more routines to hit.

Variations

- Vary the number of routines the athletes must hit. Keep in mind competition level, age, and skill level.
- Vary the reward for hitting the first routine.

➤ NO-KNEE-BEND BAR ROUTINES

Goal Encourage proper form and successful completion of an uneven bars routine.

Description The gymnast must make a bar routine with no more than five knee bends. As the gymnast performs the routine, count aloud each time she bends her knees, breaking form. Once you reach six, the gymnast stops the routine. That routine does not count toward the goal of the lesson.

Variations

- Vary the number of knee bends to be accepted.
- Instead of bent knees, consider other form or execution deductions.

➤ HEAD-UP ROUTINES

Goal Encourage good posture and presentation during a floor routine.

Description The gymnast must make a floor routine, concentrating on keeping her head up throughout the routine, especially in the choreography.

As the gymnast performs the routine, you count aloud each time she puts her head down. If the gymnast puts her head down more than five times, this routine does not count toward the goal of the lesson.

Variations

- Vary the number of acceptable "head downs."
- Instead of "head downs," consider other form or execution deductions, such as flexed feet.

Stations

Stations are a group of fitness-specific activities for gymnasts to rotate through and practice various assignments. They are meant to maximize participation and practice time on a given event. Stations should be set for one event or apparatus at a time. Ideally, there should be no more than two gymnasts per station. Gymnasts continue to practice the activity at the given station for a short time. They are directed to rotate between stations in the assigned path on your command.

For a class of 10 gymnasts, set up at least five stations. Stations can include the following elements:

- Main skills for the lesson (this may be where you are stationed)
- Lead-up skill or drill 1 (component of main skill)
- Lead-up skill or drill 2 (component of main skill that builds on lead-up skill or drill 1)
- Practice of learned skills
- Conditioning activities

Match the skills, drills, or conditioning to the objective for that lesson. There should not be more than one station that requires spotting; athletes should be able to perform the other activities on their own. Depending on the design and the skills included in the stations, you may choose to stay at one station to assist gymnasts or may move among the stations providing help and feedback. Either way, be sure all gymnasts on all stations are supervised. You should be in a position to see all the gymnasts. Do not have your back to any of the stations.

Numerous variations are possible. Change the number of stations, the rotation order, or the activities being performed. For each station, identify an easier and more difficult variation to allow the gymnasts to work at a level that is comfortable for them. Be sure to provide feedback to the gymnasts regarding all the stations.

➤ VAULT: BEGINNER LEVEL

1. Stand on block, jump (vary shapes), land on carpet square
2. 20 jump ropes
3. Hurdle with underarm circle onto springboard
4. 25 jumping jacks
5. Minimal run, hurdle onto board, jump (vary shapes), land
6. 5 push-ups
7. Squat onto mat, jump (vary shapes), land (spotted)
8. 5 handstands

➤ UNEVEN BARS: INTERMEDIATE LEVEL

1. 3 chin-ups (partner assists, medium bar)
2. Front support, 3 casts, forward roll (low bar)
3. Chin-up, pullover (spotted, low bar)
4. Chin-up, pullover (low bar)

➤ FLOOR EXERCISE: INTERMEDIATE TO ADVANCED LEVEL

1. Lunge, handstand, lunge
2. Backbend, kickover, lunge
3. Hurdle, round-off, rebound
4. Handstand forward roll from wall
5. Back walkover (incline)
6. Back handspring (trainer)
7. Back extension roll (incline)
8. Back handspring (spotted)

➤ BALANCE BEAM: ADVANCED LEVEL

1. Front support mount, stand up, landing drill
2. Locomotor skills
3. Tuck jump
4. Level changes
5. Stride leap
6. Cross handstand (spotted, medium beam)
7. Cross handstand (low beam)
8. Cartwheel (line on floor)

Stretches

Although stretching is oftentimes overlooked in gymnastics, it is a very important part of the sport; stretching both increases the range of motion and flexibility of gymnasts. It is recommended that the body and muscles to be warmed-up before performing stretching exercises. These stretching exercises can be done at the end of practice or incorporated as stations at the various events. Hold each position for 20 to 30 seconds and, when applicable, repeat on the opposite side.

STRETCHES

➤ SPLITS (HAMSTRINGS)

Straight (stride)   On the floor, extend one leg forward and one backward. Hips remain square while working the lower torso to the floor.

Middle (straddle)   With body facing forward, extend legs to either side at a 180-degree angle. Weight should be supported from the core.

➤ LUNGE WITH TWIST (QUADRICEPS/HIP FLEXORS)

From a standing position, take an exaggerated step forward. With your foot pointing straight ahead, slowly bend your front leg to get into a lunge position. Place the elbow (on the same side of the rear leg) outside of the front thigh of the lunge leg. Use this arm to press on the thigh and create rotation through the core. Without arching the low back, shift weight forward to stretch the front of the rear leg. Attempt to create a straight line from the back knee through each thigh to the front knee.

➤ WALL STRETCH (CALVES)

Lean against the wall in a lunge position with the back leg as straight as possible and front leg slightly flexed. Place both feet straight ahead. Lean into the wall and do not allow the back heel to leave the ground. You can change the angle of the stretch by slightly turning the back foot in toward the body (medial gastrocnemius) or by slightly turning the back of the foot out (lateral gastrocnemius). These stretches hit all three angles of the gastrocnemius. To focus on the soleus, perform the same stretch, slightly bending the knee of the back leg.

➤ PRETZEL (GLUTES)

Sit on the floor with the left leg flexed at the hip. Bend the left knee so it is in line with the left hip. Extend the right leg behind you until the top of your foot is touching the ground and the leg is as straight as possible. While trying to achieve level hips, lean forward slightly.

➤ FROG DOUBLE (GROIN)

Lie on the floor on your stomach. Slide both knees along the floor, bringing them as high as possible toward the chest. Extend the legs to achieve a split single position. Roll the hips internally and externally to change the angle of the stretch.

➤ OBLIQUE STRETCH (OBLIQUES)

Begin in a V-sit position with both legs stretched straight out in front of you. Bend your left leg and place your foot on the floor across your right leg. Turn to your left side and place your right elbow along your knee. Use your elbow on your thigh to press down, causing rotation as you look toward your right.

➤ STANDING HANDS BACK BAR STRETCH (SHOULDER—ANTERIOR)

Stand facing away from a bar (or mat). Reach back with the palms facing down and grab the bar. Move slightly away from the bar, flex at the knees, and slowly squat. Keep your chest up and abdominals tight.

➤ PARALLEL BARS STRETCH (CHEST)

With one hand up and the elbow flexed to 90 degrees, lean into a single bar or one side of the parallel bars or a door frame. Keep your elbow slightly below or even with your shoulders. Keep your chest upright and abdominals tight.

➤ EXTENSION AND FLEXION (WRISTS)

Grasp one hand and gently pull up (a) and press down (b).

Teaching and Shaping Skills

6

Coaching gymnastics is about teaching skills, fitness, and values to kids. It's also about coaching gymnasts before, during, and after competitions. Teaching and coaching are closely related, but there are important differences. In this chapter, we focus on principles of teaching, especially on teaching technical and tactical skills. But these principles apply to teaching values and fitness concepts as well. Armed with these principles, you will be able to design effective and efficient practices and will understand how to deal with misbehavior. Then you will be able to teach the skills that are necessary for success in gymnastics (outlined in chapters 7 through 11).

Teaching Gymnastics Skills

Many people believe that the only qualification needed for teaching a skill is to have performed it. Although it's helpful to have performed the skill, teaching it successfully requires much more than that. And even if you haven't performed the skill before, you can still learn to teach successfully with the useful acronym IDEA:

I	Introduce the skill.
D	Demonstrate the skill.
E	Explain the skill.
A	Attend to athletes practicing the skill.

Introduce the Skill

Athletes, especially those who are young and inexperienced, need to know what skill they are learning and why they are learning it. You should therefore use the following three steps every time you introduce a skill to your athletes:

1. Get your athletes' attention.
2. Name the skill.
3. Explain the importance of the skill.

Get Your Athletes' Attention

Because youngsters are easily distracted, you should do something to get their attention. Some coaches use interesting news items or stories. Others say the gymnasts' names or a key phrase. And still others simply project enthusiasm to get their athletes to listen. Whatever method you use, speak slightly above your normal volume, and look your athletes in the eyes when you speak.

Also, position gymnasts so they can see and hear you. Arrange the gymnasts with ample space between them, facing you. (Make sure they aren't looking at a distracting activity.) Then ask whether all of them can see you before you begin to speak.

Name the Skill

More than one common name may exist for the skill you are introducing, but you should decide as a staff before the start of the season which one you'll use (and then stick with it). This will help prevent confusion and will enhance communication among your gymnasts. When you introduce the new skill, call it by name several times so that the athletes automatically correlate the name with the skill in later discussions.

Explain the Importance of the Skill

As Rainer Martens, the founder of the American Sport Education Program (ASEP), has said, "The most difficult aspect of coaching is this: Coaches must learn to let athletes learn. Sport skills should be taught so they have meaning to the child, not just meaning to the coach." Although the importance of a skill may be apparent to you, your athletes may be less able to see how the skill will help them become better athletes. Give them a reason for learning the skill, and describe how the skill relates to more advanced techniques.

COACHING TIP You may want to write out in detail each skill you will teach. This can help clarify what you will say and how you will demonstrate and teach each skill to your gymnasts.

Demonstrate the Skill

The demonstration step is the most important part of teaching a sport skill to athletes who may never have done anything closely resembling the skill. They need a picture, not just words, so they can see how the skill is performed. Ask one of your gymnasts or use video or pictures to demonstrate the skill.

These tips will help make your demonstrations more effective:

- Use correct form.
- Show the skill several times.
- Slow the action, if possible, during one or two performances so athletes can see every movement involved in the skill.
- Show the skill at different angles, if possible, so your athletes can get a full perspective of it.

Explain the Skill

Athletes learn more effectively when they're given a brief explanation of the skill along with the demonstration. You should use simple terms and, if possible, relate the skill to previously learned skills. Ask your gymnasts whether they understand your description. A good technique is to ask them to repeat your explanation. Ask questions such as "What are you going to do first?" and "Then what?" If athletes look confused or uncertain, you should repeat your explanation and demonstration. If possible, use different words so your gymnasts get a chance to try to understand the skill from a different perspective.

Complex skills are often better understood when they are explained in more manageable parts. For instance, if you want to teach your gymnasts how to perform a handstand forward roll, you might take the following steps:

1. Show your athletes a correct performance of the entire skill.
2. Break down the skill, and point out its components.
3. Have athletes perform each of the component skills you have already taught them, such as the forward roll and kick to handstand.
4. After athletes have demonstrated their ability to perform the separate parts of the skill in sequence, reexplain the entire skill.
5. Have athletes practice the skill in a sequence with other steps or skills.

Young athletes have short attention spans, and a long demonstration or explanation of a skill may cause them to lose focus. Therefore, you should spend no more than a few minutes altogether on the introduction, demonstration, and explanation phases. Then involve the gymnasts in drills or games that call on them to perform the skill.

COACHING TIP   Improvements in technology have brought new demonstration methods to the gym. A variety of gymnastics DVDs are on the market; if you're fortunate enough to have access to a portable DVD player, consider using it as a tool to show gymnasts how to perform skills. This method can be especially useful if you have difficulty demonstrating a particular skill or locating someone who can demonstrate it for you. DVDs are very effective with older gymnasts, who are better able to transfer the skills they see on the screen to their own performance.

How to Run Your Drills

Before running a drill that teaches technique, you should do the following:

- Name the drill.
- Explain the skill or skills to be taught.
- Demonstrate the drill.
- Explain what the drill will accomplish.
- Tell the gymnasts how many repetitions of the drill to complete and if they should practice other drills intermittently.

Once the drill has been introduced and repeated a few times in this manner, you will find that merely calling out the name of the drill is sufficient; your gymnasts will automatically know what to do to run the drill and practice the skill.

Attend to Athletes Practicing the Skill

If the skill you selected is within your athletes' capabilities and you have done an effective job of introducing, demonstrating, and explaining it, your athletes should be ready to attempt the skill. Some gymnasts, especially those in younger age groups, may need to be physically guided (e.g., spotted) through the movements during their first few attempts. Walking unsure gymnasts through the skill in this way will help them gain confidence to perform the skill on their own.

Your teaching duties, though, don't end when all your gymnasts have demonstrated that they understand how to perform a skill. In fact, your teaching role is just beginning as you help your gymnasts improve their skills. A significant part of your teaching consists of closely observing your athletes' hit-and-miss trial performances. You will shape athletes' skills by detecting errors and correcting them using positive feedback. Keep in mind that your positive feedback will have a great influence on your gymnasts' motivation to practice and improve their performances.

Remember, too, that some gymnasts may need individual instruction. So set aside a time before, during, or after practice to give individual help.

Helping Athletes Improve Skills

After you have successfully taught your gymnasts the fundamentals of a skill, your focus will be on helping them improve the skill. Athletes learn skills and improve on them at different rates, so don't get frustrated if progress seems slow. Instead, help them improve by shaping their skills and detecting and correcting errors.

Shaping Athletes' Skills

One of your principal teaching duties is to reward positive effort or behavior—in terms of successful skill execution—when you see it. A gymnast properly performs a back walkover on the balance beam, and you immediately say, "Beautiful back walkover! I especially like your lunge at the end. Great job!" This, plus a smile and a thumbs-up gesture, goes a long way toward reinforcing that technique in that gymnast. However, sometimes you may have a long dry spell before you see correct techniques to reinforce. It's difficult to reward athletes when they don't execute skills correctly. How can you shape their skills if this is the case?

Shaping skills takes practice on your athletes' part and patience on yours. Expect your gymnasts to make errors. Telling the gymnast who performed the proper back walkover that she did a good job doesn't ensure that she'll have the same success next time. Seeing inconsistency in your athletes' technique can be frustrating. It's even more challenging to stay positive when your athletes repeatedly perform a skill incorrectly or show a lack of enthusiasm for learning. It can certainly be frustrating to see athletes who seemingly don't heed your advice continue to make the same mistakes.

Although it is normal to get frustrated sometimes when teaching skills, part of successful coaching is controlling this frustration. Instead of getting upset, use these six guidelines for shaping skills:

1. Think small initially.

Reward the first signs of behavior that approximate what you want. Then reward closer and closer approximations of the desired behavior. In short, use your reward power to shape the behavior you seek.

2. Break skills into small steps.

Before performing an entire skill, a gymnast needs to understand how to do each step within the skill using correct form. For instance, in learning a proper back walkover, one of your gymnasts has good flexibility and completes the skill nicely, but she doesn't keep her body tight and fully stretched at the end, which affects the ending of the skill and makes it difficult for her to stay on the beam. Reinforce the correct techniques of the back walkover, and teach her how to keep her muscles contracted throughout the entire skill and keep her arms tight against her ears at the end so that she stays on the beam. Once she masters this, shift the focus to getting her to finish in the proper lunge position while remaining on the beam.

3. Develop one component of a skill at a time.

Don't try to shape two components of a skill at once. For example, in vaulting, gymnasts must learn to run and hurdle onto the board, rebound from the board, and perform a skill over the vault table. Gymnasts should focus first on one aspect (run and hurdle), then on another (rebound), and then on the remaining components of the skill. Gymnasts who have problems mastering a skill are often trying to improve two or more components at once. You should help these athletes isolate a single component.

4. Use reinforcement only occasionally, and only for the best examples.

By focusing only on the best examples, you will help athletes continue to improve once they've mastered the basics. Using only occasional reinforcement during practice allows athletes to have more active time instead of having to constantly stop and listen to your instructions. Gymnastics skills are best learned through a lot of repetition, such as drills and competitive activities, and you should make the best use of team practice time by allowing the athletes to have as much training time as possible.

5. Relax your reward standards.

As gymnasts learn a new skill or learn to combine two or more skills into one action, a temporary deterioration of previously learned skills may occur, and you may need to relax your expectations. For example, a gymnast who has learned how to perform a rebound straight jump off the vaulting board is now learning a jump to handstand (onto a raised mat surface). While learning the new skill and getting the rhythm down, the gymnast's execution of all components may be poor. A similar degeneration of skills may occur during growth spurts while the coordination of muscles, tendons, and ligaments catches up to the growth of bones. As a coach, you need to remain patient as a gymnast is learning something new.

6. Go back to the basics.

If, however, a well-learned skill degenerates for long, you may need to restore it by going back to the basics. If necessary, have the athlete practice the skill using a low-pressure activity. For example, let the gymnast practice with a lower mat stack, and raise the height only when the gymnast is comfortable with his technique.

COACHING TIP   For older age groups or athletes with advanced skills, you can ask athletes to self-coach. With the proper guidance and a positive team environment, athletes can think about how they perform a skill and how they might be able to perform it better. Self-coaching is best done at practice, where an athlete can experiment with learning new skills.

Detecting and Correcting Errors

Good coaches recognize that athletes make two types of errors: learning errors and performance errors. Learning errors occur because athletes don't know how to perform a skill; that is, they have not yet developed the correct motor pattern in the brain to perform a particular skill. Performance errors are made not because athletes don't know how to execute the skill but because they have made a mistake in executing what they do know. There is no easy way to know whether an athlete is making learning or performance errors; part of the art of coaching is being able to sort out which type of error each mistake is.

The process of helping your athletes correct errors begins with observing and evaluating their performances to determine if the mistakes are learning or performance errors. Carefully watch your gymnasts to see if they routinely make the errors in both practice and competition settings or if the errors tend to occur only at meets. If the latter is the case, then your gymnasts are making performance errors. For performance errors, you need to look for the reasons your gymnasts are not performing as well as they can; perhaps they are nervous, or maybe they get distracted by the meet setting. If the mistakes are learning errors, then you need to help the gymnasts learn the skill, which is the focus of this section.

When correcting learning errors, there is no substitute for your own mastery of the skill. The better you understand a skill—not only how it is performed correctly but also what causes learning errors—the more helpful you will be in correcting your athletes' mistakes.

One of the most common coaching mistakes is providing inaccurate feedback and advice on how to correct errors. Don't rush into error correction; wrong feedback or poor advice will hurt the learning process more than no feedback or advice at all. If you are uncertain about the cause of the problem or how to correct it, you should continue to observe and analyze until you are more certain. As a rule, you should see the error repeated more than just occasionally before attempting to correct it.

Correct One Error at a Time

Suppose Megan, one of your more experienced gymnasts, is having trouble with her pullover on bars. She does not pull her chin close enough to the bar, which makes it difficult to lift her hips and legs over and around the bar. What do you do?

First, you must decide which error to correct first—athletes learn more effectively when they attempt to correct one error at a time. Determine whether one error is causing the other; if so, have the athlete correct that error first because it may eliminate the other error (which is the case with Megan). However, if neither error is causing the other, athletes should first correct the error that is easiest to correct and will bring the greatest improvement when remedied. Note that improvement in one area may even motivate the athlete to correct other errors.

Use Positive Feedback to Correct Errors

The positive approach to correcting errors includes emphasizing what to do instead of what not to do. Use praise, rewards, and encouragement to correct errors. Acknowledge correct performance as well as efforts to improve. By using positive feedback, you can help your athletes feel good about themselves and promote a strong desire to achieve.

When you're working with one gymnast at a time, the positive approach to correcting errors includes four steps:

1. **Praise effort and correct performance.**

Praise the gymnast for trying to perform a skill correctly and for performing any parts of it correctly. Praise the gymnast immediately after he performs the skill, if possible. Keep the praise simple: "Good try," "Way to hustle," "Good form," or "That's the way to follow through." You can also use nonverbal feedback, such as smiling, clapping your hands, or using any facial or body expression that shows approval.

Make sure you're sincere with your praise. Don't indicate that an athlete's effort was good when it wasn't. Usually an athlete knows when he has made a sincere effort to perform the skill correctly, and he will perceive undeserved praise for what it is—untruthful feedback to make him feel good. Likewise, don't indicate that an athlete's performance was correct when it wasn't.

2. Give simple and precise feedback to correct errors.

Don't burden a gymnast with a long or detailed explanation of how to correct an error. Give just enough feedback so that the gymnast can correct one error at a time. Before giving feedback, recognize that some athletes readily accept it immediately after the error; others will respond better if you slightly delay the correction.

For errors that are complicated to explain and difficult to correct, you should try the following:

- Explain and demonstrate what the athlete should have done. Do not demonstrate what the athlete did wrong.
- Explain the cause (or causes) of the error if it isn't obvious.
- Explain why you are recommending the correction you have selected if it's not obvious.

3. Make sure the athlete understands your feedback.

If the gymnast doesn't understand your feedback, she won't be able to correct the error. Ask her to repeat the feedback and to explain and demonstrate how it will be used. If the gymnast can't do this, you should be patient and present your feedback again. Then have the gymnast repeat the feedback after you're finished.

4. Provide an environment that motivates the athlete to improve.

Your gymnasts won't always be able to correct their errors immediately, even if they do understand your feedback. Encourage them to stick with it when they seem discouraged or when corrections are difficult. For more difficult corrections, remind gymnasts that it will take time, and that the improvement will happen only if they work at it. Encourage those athletes with little self-confidence. Saying something like "You're getting your chin closer to the bar today; with practice and conditioning, you'll become stronger and be able to perform your pullover without a problem" can motivate an athlete to continue to refine her strength and skills on the uneven bars.

Other athletes may be very self-motivated and need little help from you in this area; with these athletes, you can practically ignore step 4 when correcting an error. Although motivation comes from within, you should still try to provide an environment of positive instruction and encouragement to help such gymnasts improve.

A final note on correcting errors: Sports such as gymnastics provide unique challenges in this endeavor because you might be working with several athletes simultaneously. How do you provide individual feedback in a group setting using a positive approach? Instead of yelling (and embarrassing a gymnast) during the middle of an activity, you should pull aside a gymnast who is having trouble and then provide one-on-one feedback. This type of feedback has several advantages:

- The gymnast will be more receptive to the one-on-one feedback.
- The other athletes are still active and still practicing skills, and they are unable to hear your discussion.

- Because the rest of the group are still practicing, you'll feel compelled to make your comments simple and concise—which is more helpful to the gymnast.

This doesn't mean you can't use the group setting to give specific, positive feedback. You can do so to emphasize correct group and individual performances. Use this group feedback approach only for positive statements, though. Keep any negative feedback for individual discussions.

Dealing With Misbehavior

Young athletes will misbehave at times; it's only natural. Following are two ways you can respond to misbehavior: through extinction or discipline.

Extinction

Ignoring misbehavior—neither rewarding nor disciplining it—is called *extinction*. This can be effective under certain circumstances. In some situations, disciplining young people's misbehavior only encourages them to act up further because of the recognition they get. Ignoring misbehavior teaches youngsters that it is not worth your attention.

Sometimes, though, you cannot wait for a behavior to fizzle out. When an athlete causes danger to herself or others, or disrupts the activities of others, you need to take immediate action. Tell the offending athlete that the behavior must stop and that discipline will follow if it doesn't. If the athlete doesn't stop misbehaving after the warning, you should use discipline.

Extinction also doesn't work well when a misbehavior is self-rewarding. For example, you may be able to keep from grimacing if a youngster kicks you in the shin, but even so, the youngster still knows you were hurt. Therein lies the reward. In these circumstances, it is also necessary to discipline the athlete for the undesirable behavior.

Extinction works best in situations where athletes are seeking recognition through mischievous behaviors, clowning around, or grandstanding. Usually, if you are patient, their failure to get your attention will cause the behavior to disappear. However, you must be alert that you don't extinguish desirable behavior. When youngsters do something well, they expect to be positively reinforced. Not rewarding them will likely cause them to discontinue the desired behavior.

Discipline

Some educators say we should never discipline young people but should only reinforce their positive behaviors. These educators argue that discipline does not work, creates hostility, and sometimes causes avoidance behaviors that may be more unwholesome than the original problem behavior. It is true that discipline does not always work and that it can create problems when used ineffectively;

however, when used appropriately, discipline is effective in eliminating undesirable behaviors without creating other undesirable consequences. You should consider using discipline because it is difficult to guide athletes through positive reinforcement and extinction alone. Discipline is part of a positive approach when these guidelines are followed:

- Discipline athletes in a corrective way to help them improve now and in the future. Never use discipline to retaliate or to make yourself feel better.

- Impose discipline in an impersonal way when athletes break team rules or otherwise misbehave. Shouting at or scolding athletes indicates that your attitude is one of revenge.

- Once a good rule has been agreed on, ensure that athletes who violate it experience the unpleasant consequences of their misbehavior. Don't wave discipline threateningly over their heads. Warn an athlete once before disciplining, then just do it.

- Be consistent in administering discipline.

- Don't discipline using consequences that may cause you guilt. If you can't think of an appropriate consequence right away, tell the athlete you will talk with him after you think about it. You might consider involving the athlete in designing a consequence.

- Once the discipline is completed, don't make athletes think they are "in the doghouse." Always make them believe they are valued members of the team.

- Make sure that what you think is discipline isn't perceived by the athlete as positive reinforcement; for instance, keeping an athlete out of doing a certain activity or portion of the training session may be just what the athlete wanted.

- Never discipline athletes for making mistakes when they are performing.

- Never use physical activity or conditioning—running laps or doing push-ups—as discipline. To do so only causes athletes to resent physical activity, something we want them to learn to enjoy throughout their lives.

- Use discipline sparingly. Constant discipline and criticism causes athletes to turn their interests elsewhere and to resent you as well.

COACHING TIP Involve older athletes in the process of setting team rules and the consequences for breaking them. Gymnasts who are 12 or older are capable of brainstorming ideas about discipline for common situations such as being late for practice, criticizing another gymnast, or talking back to the coach. Once you've agreed on a list of rules and consequences, each athlete should sign an agreement to cement her willingness to abide by them.

Gymnastics Basics

7

Gymnastics is a sport filled with high-powered tumbling, gravity-defying routines, and breath-catching moments. These are the elements of gymnastics that you see on television and have heard about throughout the years. However, none of this could happen without a starting point. Gymnasts don't begin their training with high-difficulty elements and Olympic-level routines; they begin with the basics. Developmentally, it is very difficult to perform at a high level without proper introductory training.

Basic skills and techniques taught at the early levels lay the foundation for higher levels of training and should be mastered before advancing in the sport. Unlike other sports requiring that only a few skills be mastered, gymnastics has hundreds, maybe thousands, of skills to be learned and perfected. All the gymnastics disciplines incorporate fundamental gymnastics movements and skills into their developmental programs. This chapter covers basic gymnastics terms, movements, body positions, and concepts important to early gymnastics training.

COACHING TIP Fundamental information about gymnastics movements and skills includes biomechanical principles, movement patterns, body shapes and positions, and gymnastics terminology. As a coach, you need to understand these fundamentals so that you can teach your athletes the correct execution of skills, develop effective lesson plans and progressions, and provide feedback to athletes.

Movement: The Foundation of Gymnastics Skills

To teach the skills of gymnastics correctly, you have to understand how the body of a gymnast moves and functions. Gymnastics involves skills with unique technical requirements, but often skills can be grouped into categories with similar underlying movements. An introduction to basic biomechanical concepts helps coaches understand skill techniques and performance, identify ideal positions, select and implement skill progressions, and therefore enable the ultimate success of the gymnasts. An understanding of fundamental movements also helps establish links and similarities between different skills on the different apparatus.

Dominant Movement Patterns

Gymnastics skills can be classified into six dominant movement patterns: landings, statics, locomotions, rotations, springs, and swings. The development of awareness and competency within each movement pattern should be the focus of a recreation-based gymnastics program. Each movement pattern is defined here, and additional information and examples of skills are presented in later chapters.

- *Landings:* Landings involve absorbing force to stop movement. Landing is the most important skill in gymnastics because it is the most frequently performed, and proper landings ensure safety.

- *Statics:* Statics involve any position where the center of gravity is above the base of support and is stable. These include positions where you are balanced and stable on various body parts. Examples of bases of support are the feet, hands, shoulders, and buttocks.

- *Locomotions:* Locomotion, or traveling, is achieved by the transfer of weight from one part of the body to either the same part or another part in succession. This is normally brought about by transferring weight onto one or both feet. Examples of locomotions are running, skipping, hopping, and leaping.

- *Rotations:* Rotations are body movements around an internal axis. Types of rotations include vertical (rotation around the vertical axis that runs head to toe), horizontal (rotation around the horizontal axis that runs from one side of the waist to the other), and anterior–posterior (rotation around the anterior–posterior axis running from front to back).

- *Springs:* Springs involve rapid displacement of the body, such as the takeoff from both legs in jumping and the spring from both hands in a front handspring.

- *Swings:* Swings are rotations around an external axis such as the uneven bars or high bar.

Center of Gravity

Also known as center of mass, the midpoint or average location of all material in an object, a gymnast's center of gravity is located approximately an inch (2.5 cm) below the navel and about halfway from front to back. However, the center of gravity will change with certain body movements or shapes. For example, the center of gravity rises when a gymnast's arms are raised overhead. Center of gravity is important when teaching gymnastics skills because many of the basic skills require gymnasts to rotate around their center of gravity. In addition to serving as the axis of rotation, the center of gravity affects balance and stability. If a gymnast is tall (and therefore has a relatively high center of gravity), it will be more difficult for her to balance while standing on relevé on a beam because her center of gravity is far away from her base of support. If a gymnast is short, it will be easier for her to balance.

Gymnastics Positions and Movements

The body positions and movements defined and demonstrated in this chapter will help you communicate effectively with your gymnasts and other coaches. By knowing these, you will demonstrate knowledge of the sport and professionalism as a coach. There are thousands of gymnastics positions and movements. These are some of the basics to get you started. These movements and positions are incorporated into many gymnastics skills. For a list of terms, including those mentioned in this section, see the glossary on page 254.

General Body Positions

The position or posture of the body is one of the most important aspects in regard to successfully acquiring proper gymnastics skills and landings. The proper position of the body is one of proper alignment. In a neutral standing position, the stomach is pulled in, the buttocks are tucked under, the shoulders are down, the arms are relaxed at the sides of body, and the head is straight (neutral) with eyes facing straight ahead. Although various parts of the body will change position in gymnastics, proper alignment of the body must still be maintained. The following photos show changes in body positions while emphasizing proper body posture (alignment).

➤ HEAD POSITIONS

 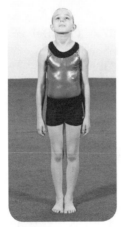  

Head neutral
Neck long, chin lifted, eyes facing forward.

Head back
Head tilted away from chest.

Head forward
Chin tucked to chest.

Head turned
Chin over shoulder.

➤ HIP POSITIONS

Hips neutral
Hips and
shoulders aligned
and parallel to
each other.

Hips twisted
Shoulders not
aligned with hips.

Hips square
Hips aligned with
shoulders as well
as in line with
any apparatus
the gymnast
is performing
on (such as the
beam or bar).

Hips open
Hips extended;
no segmentation
or pike of the
body. A straight
line can be drawn
from the rib cage
through the knee.

➤ ARM AND SHOULDER POSITIONS

Arm Positions

Straight Extended.   **Bent** Flexed.

Rounded Arms slightly
bent, with fingertips
close together.

Arm Levels

High   Arms up by ears, shoulder-width apart.

Middle   Arms parallel to the floor, either out in front (front middle) or to the sides of the body (side middle).

Low   Arms down by sides.

Arm Widths

Close together

Shoulder-width apart

Wide   Greater than shoulder-width apart.

Arm Opposition

Arms are in opposition to legs   Right arm is forward while left leg is forward; left arm is back while right leg is back.

Shoulder Positions

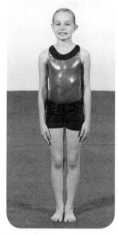   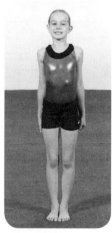

Neutral
Shoulders pressed down, relaxed.

Elevated
Shoulders up close to ears.

Forward
Hollow chest.

Backward
Shoulder blades pinched together.

➤ WRIST, HAND, AND FINGER POSITIONS

Wrists

Neutral Straight
position.

Extended

Flexed

Hands

Supporting position

Grasping position

Fingers

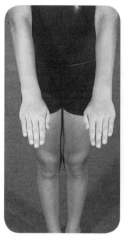 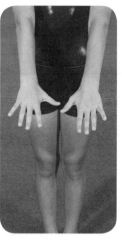  

| Together | Spread apart | Pointed away from body | Pointed toward body |

➤ KNEE, LEG, AND FOOT POSITIONS

Knees

Straight

Bent

Legs

Together

Apart

Feet

Pointed Extended.

Flexed

Legs and Feet

Parallel

Turned out

Turned in

Relative Body Positions

Numerous positions are used in gymnastics where the body (torso) has a different relationship to the legs or the apparatus. Understanding these positions is important when performing certain skills or movements.

➤ SQUAT

Using the balls of the feet for support with the knees and hips flexed so that the buttocks is near, but not touching, the heels and the torso is erect.

➤ TUCK

The body is curled up in a ball; the upper body is flexed forward at the hips, and the knees are flexed and pulled up to the chest.

➤ ARCH

The upper and lower parts of the back are stretched backward, forming a curve.

➤ HOLLOW

Beginning from a stretched body position, contracting the chest and abdomen inward with a pelvic tilt and bringing the shoulders forward. The gymnast should have a rounded upper back.

➤ STRADDLE

A position in which the legs are straight and extended sideward.

➤ LAYOUT

The whole body is extended (no bent segments). Also called straight or stretched position.

➤ PIKE

The body is flexed forward at the hips while the legs remain straight.

➤ INVERTED

Any position in which the lower body is moved into a position above the upper body.

➤ PRONE

Lying facedown on the floor.

➤ SUPINE

Lying flat on the back.

➤ FRONT SUPPORT

Arms are straight and extended in front of the body.

➤ REAR SUPPORT

Arms are straight and extended behind the body.

Standing Body Positions and Balances

Understanding the correct body position (alignment) in both standing positions and balances allows the gymnast to maintain proper positions from beginning to ending poses in routines as well as proper stance upon landing.

➤ STRAIGHT STAND

Standing with the feet together, either parallel or turned out 45 degrees, legs straight, abdomen tight, rib cage lifted, arms at sides, and head erect (a). When the arms are extended up by the ears, this position is called a stretched stand or finish position (b). The body should form a straight line.

➤ GYMNASTICS POINT (TENDU)

Beginning with a stretched body position, placing one foot forward with the leg straight and toe pointed, lightly touching the floor. The extended leg can be turned out. The other leg should remain straight and support the body weight. The hips are square. This is often used as a starting position for gymnastics skills.

➤ PLIÉ

Bending the knees with feet flat on the floor and the body straight and upright *(a)*. Demi-pliés (slight bend of the knees, *b*) are important for safe landings and takeoffs.

➤ RELEVÉ

Standing in a straight position on the balls of the feet (on toes).

➤ COUPÉ

Standing on one leg with the free leg bent and toes pointed, with the big toe at the ankle of the support leg. The knee of the free leg can face forward or sideward.

➤ PASSÉ

Standing on one leg with the free leg bent and toes pointed, with the big toe at the knee of the support leg. The knee of the free leg can face forward or sideward. The thigh (upper leg) of the free leg should be horizontal.

➤ FRONT ATTITUDE

Standing on one leg, the free leg lifted forward so the thigh is horizontal and the leg is turned out, with the knee bent slightly.

Movements

Following are general movements used often in gymnastics.

➤ SALTO

Better known as a somersault, a skill where the lower body rotates over the upper body. It can be performed backward, forward, and sideward.

➤ LUNGE

Position in which one leg is forward and flexed (approximately 45 degrees) and the other leg is straight and extended backward. The body is stretched and upright, with weight over the flexed leg. A lunge is often used as an initiation or finish position for gymnastics skills.

➤ HURDLE

A long, low, powerful skip step that may be preceded by one or more running steps. Generally, a hurdle is used to generate power into a round-off tumbling series or as a step onto the vaulting springboard.

➤ CRAB STAND

A flat, tabletop-like position with feet and hands flat on the floor and the abdomen up. Hips should be open and torso extended and as close to parallel to the floor as possible. This is a skill progression for a bridge.

➤ BRIDGE

An arched position with the feet and hands flat on the floor and the abdomen up. This position is achieved by lying on the back and pushing up onto the hands and feet.

➤ BACKBEND

From a stand, arching backward to place the hands on the floor to form a bridge.

➤ SPLIT

Position where the legs are extended 180 degrees on both sides of the torso. Stride splits have one leg forward and one leg in back of the torso (a). Straddle splits have the right leg extending right and the left leg extending left of the body (b).

➤ HANDSTAND

Hands are flat on the floor, shoulder-width apart, and the body is completely extended and straight, legs together. Leg positions can also vary: stride, stag, straddle, or any combination of these.

Teaching Gymnastics Skills

When teaching the basics of gymnastics, there are a few ways to approach each skill. You can adapt the training method based on the skill being taught, the competitive level, and the experience of the gymnast. The three methods described here—lead-up skills, drills, and progressions—are effective ways to teach gymnastics skills. By properly teaching gymnastics skills, you can foster greater learning opportunities, more success, and a safer environment. This is also discussed in chapter 5.

Lead-Up Skills

Lead-up skills involve breaking a skill into manageable parts. The gymnasts practice the parts of the skill and then progress to putting the parts together to complete the full skill. This is also referred to as the part–whole method. Lead-up skills help gymnasts learn how to break down difficult skills into smaller parts and learn each part before trying to master the entire skill all at once.

An example of a lead-up skill for a backward roll is rocking backward (figure 7.1, a-b). The gymnast begins in a squat position and rolls backward, with the legs in tuck position and the head tucked forward (chin to chest). She rolls back until her shoulders touch the floor and her buttocks is raised off the floor. The gymnast should also practice placing her hands on the floor by her shoulders with the palms down and fingers pointing toward the shoulders. This lead-up skill is the beginning of the backward roll.

FIGURE 7.1   Lead-up skill: rocking backward.

Drills

Drills are activities that mimic certain actions of a skill. They are important in teaching gymnastics because they help the gymnast develop strength, flexibility, and body awareness to better perform the complete skill. Drills allow for greater repetition, which is important when teaching a new skill because it can help develop proper technique by focusing on the raw elements of a skill and also creating good habits when executing a skill.

To illustrate the concept of a drill, consider a backward roll on an incline (wedge) mat (figure 7.2, *a-c*). Using an incline mat makes the skill easier for the gymnast and allows her to feel the complete movement and develop coordination and strength before doing the skill on the floor.

FIGURE 7.2   Drill: backward roll on incline mat.

Progressions

Teaching skills in a step-by-step fashion is called a progression. This allows athletes to learn and master basic skills first before moving to more advanced skills. Use of progressions also allows for maximum development, advancement, and success of athletes.

For example, gymnasts should learn how to consistently perform a backward roll (figure 7.3, *a-c*) before learning a back extension roll (figure 7.4, *a-d*). The backward roll is a critical component and therefore serves as a skill progression for the back extension roll.

FIGURE 7.3   Progression: backward roll.

FIGURE 7.4   Progression: back extension roll.

Landing and Falling

Landing properly and knowing how to fall are both key aspects of injury prevention in the sport of gymnastics. These are prerequisite skills for gymnastics performance, and gymnasts should be continually educated in these areas. Education and reminders should be built into lesson plans and used for each apparatus.

Landing Properly

Landing properly should be automatic and a natural position for all gymnasts. Proper landing technique helps reduce the forces of landings. Safe landing technique (figure 7.5) includes the following:

1. Knees slightly bent to absorb the impact of landing
   - No straight legs on the landing
   - No squat position on the landing
2. Straight spine to keep the neck stable and prevent falling forward
   - No arch in the lower back
   - No bending forward at the waist

FIGURE 7.5   Safe landing technique.

3. Arms extended to the front, straight and level with the heart in order to keep chest up on the landing

Learning How to Fall

Falls are commonplace in the gymnastics environment, especially as athletes learn new skills. Teach your gymnasts how to fall properly by demonstrating and practicing safety rolls. Safety rolls allow gymnasts to absorb the impact of a fall over a greater area of their bodies.

A safety roll, also known as a recovery roll, should be performed if a gymnast is off balance (figure 7.6, *a-c*). The gymnast should roll in the direction she is traveling—forward or diagonally (shoulder roll), backward, or sideways—instead of trying to immediately stop her momentum.

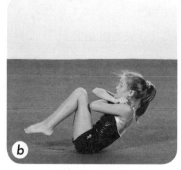

FIGURE 7.6   Safety roll.

Tell your gymnasts to do the following when falling:

1. Make fists with the hands.
2. Pull the arms in toward the body and across the chest.
3. Roll in a tucked position.

Note: Rolls can also be done with the arms overhead (i.e., halo shape).

Depending on the age and level of the gymnast, different methods may be employed to structure gymnastics classes and teach gymnastics skills.

Developmental gymnastics activities are designed for young children. These activities simulate major movement patterns and appeal to children's natural desire to play and explore. Developmental gymnastics teaches skills step by step. This not only is the safest way to teach gymnastics but also is fun for the gymnasts because it allows them to build on previously learned skills and experience success along the way. Developmental gymnastics helps gymnasts develop physically (developing strength, flexibility, balance, coordination, and motor skills), mentally (following directions, learning terminology, and focusing on activities), and socially (playing with other gymnasts, separating from parents, taking turns, and developing self-confidence).

Sequential gymnastics was originally developed for school-age children in physical education and gymnastics classes. It includes skills and movement sequences that represent the primary movement categories. Sequential gymnastics groups like elements together. The program is very flexible, allowing coaches and teachers to select skills from various movement categories based on the availability of equipment, class size, gymnast experience, curriculum goals, and so on.

Beginning with this chapter through chapter 11, we explore basic gymnastics movement categories and skills on the floor, vault, bars, and balance beam. These are preparatory or introductory skills that will prepare gymnasts in all the gymnastics disciplines for advancement into intermediate gymnastics and on to the Junior Olympic competitive program. These movements and skills are presented in a progressive manner from basic to intermediate A to intermediate B to advanced and were originally developed for school-age participants, but they can easily be adapted for preschool children as well. Basic skills are skills the gymnast should experience first. At the intermediate A level, the gymnast is introduced to skills that are based on those basic skills. The intermediate B level is a more difficult skill level, and the gymnast must make use of previously learned skills as well as possibly achieve a specific level of fitness. Advanced skills not only require knowledge of basic and intermediate-level skills, but they also require certain levels of strength and flexibility.

Locomotions

The term *locomotion* refers to the act of traveling, or transferring weight from one part of the body to another. Locomotions include actions such as walking, running, skipping, and other movements that help children develop agility, coordination, and strength and that let them have fun being active. Gymnastics is a great activity in which to learn these valuable skills, and these types of movements are fabulous for introductory classes and preschool children.

COACHING TIP   These movements can easily be turned into games, relay races, or other fun activities.

➤ WALKING

Basic Practice walking in different ways and directions such as forward (a), backward, sideward (lateral), and in relevé (on toe, b).

➤ RUNNING

Basic Practice running, again in various directions including forward, backward, and sideward. Also try running on one foot.

➤ SKIPPING

Basic   This is similar to a running motion, with the addition of a hop as one foot comes off the ground. Alternate feet.

➤ CHASSÉ

Intermediate A   Step forward and spring slightly off the floor. The legs briefly come together in the air. Land on the back leg with the front leg lifted slightly in preparation for the next movement. Perform the activity moving forward (using both legs as lead legs) and sideward.

➤ GRAPEVINE

Intermediate A   From a stand, step one foot to the side, then move the other foot behind the first, then move the first foot to the side again (in the same direction), and then bring the second foot in front of the first. Repeat and go in both directions. This can be done in a walking motion or faster.

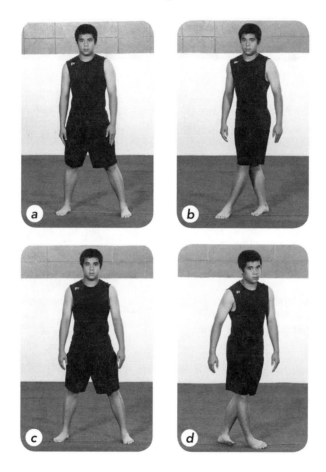

COACHING TIP   For more difficult movements, combine different locomotions together or change sides or directions. Basic locomotor skills can also be done on a strip on the floor or on the low beam to add difficulty and a change of pace.

Animal Movements

Animal movements can be a fun way to exercise the gymnasts' imaginations as well as help them move in different ways, simulate gymnastics-type activities, and develop strength and coordination. Animal movements are best for more beginning-level gymnasts.

ANIMAL MOVEMENTS

➤ BEAR WALK

Basic With hands and feet on the floor, raise the buttocks in the air and walk on all fours (hands and feet). Move forward and backward.

➤ CRAB WALK

Basic Start by sitting on the floor. Place the hands flat behind you, with fingers pointed outward or toward the buttocks. Bend the knees and place the feet flat on the floor, with your belly facing upward. Placing weight on the hands and feet, pick the buttocks up off the floor so the body is supported in a tabletop-like position. The trunk should be flat and as close to horizontal to the floor as possible. Move forward, backward, and sideward.

➤ BUNNY HOP

Basic   Standing on two feet, raise the arms above the head and perform small bounces traveling forward. Keep the arms above the head until completed. Bunny hops can also be done traveling backward.

➤ SPIDER WALK

Intermediate A   Starting in a front support (push-up) position, move the left arm and leg out to the side, and then move the right arm and leg in the same direction to get back to the front support position. Repeat and go in both directions.

➤ INCHWORM

Intermediate A   From a stand, reach the hands down to the floor near the feet. Walk the hands out in front until the body is in a front support position. Then walk the feet in toward the hands until they are almost touching. Repeat, walking the hands out and then the feet in.

Statics

Statics include those skills where a gymnast's center of gravity is above the base of support and the gymnast is balanced and stable. These types of movements and skills can help gymnasts develop an understanding of various body positions as well as improve strength, flexibility, and balance. Statics are common elements in the performance of other skills, and can be done with the feet, the hands, or another body part as the base of support. Statics should be practiced at all gymnastics levels.

STATICS

Upright Balances

The term *upright* refers to a position where the head is above the trunk of the body and the feet. The following skills are forms of upright balances.

➤ V-SIT

Basic   Sit on the floor and slide the feet toward the buttocks (tuck position), with the hands on the floor next to the buttocks. Lift the legs to a V position, hold momentarily, and then lift the hands to an extended position sideward while the legs are still in the V position. Balance for two seconds.

➤ FRONT SUPPORT

Basic   From a prone position, push up on the hands and the balls of the feet, with the body in a straight line. Also known as a push-up position.

➤ REAR SUPPORT

Basic   From a sitting position, push up on the hands (hands facing outward or toward the buttocks) and feet, with the body in a straight line.

➤ SIDE SUPPORT

Basic Lie on one side, stack the feet, and place a bent elbow underneath the shoulder. Lift up from the hips onto the elbow and edge of the bottom foot (not the ankle), forming a straight line with the body.

➤ LUNGE

Intermediate A Step one foot forward to a stand in a lunge position, with the knee of the front leg flexed. The head is up with eyes focused forward, the shoulders and hips are square, the back leg is straight, both feet are turned out slightly, the arms are stretched upward by the ears, and slightly more weight is over the front leg than the back leg.

➤ ARABESQUE

Intermediate A Stand on both feet, keeping the upper body vertical and extended. Lift one leg backward and upward (6 to 12 inches [15 to 30 cm] or higher), maintaining a vertical curve in the body. Arms are stretched out to the sides or low near the body.

➤ SCALE

Intermediate A In a scale, the upper body is lowered (shoulders to about hip height) as the back leg is raised to horizontal or above. Arms are stretched out to the sides or low near the body.

➤ SIDE SCALE

Intermediate A Stand on both feet. Lift one leg sideward while simultaneously lowering the upper body to the opposite side. Try to hold the leg at or above horizontal. Arms can be stretched to the sides or low near the body.

➤ FRONT-LEG BALANCE

Intermediate A Keeping the base leg straight, raise one leg forward and upward to a 45-degree angle or higher. Maintain a straight vertical position with the trunk of the body. The lifted leg should be straight and turned out slightly. Arms can be stretched to the sides or low near the body.

105

➤ CROSS-LEGGED HAND SUPPORT

Intermediate B Sit cross-legged with the hands on the floor by the hips. Lift to a support with the buttocks and legs off the floor by extending the arms (the feet do not need to come off the floor on the first few attempts).

➤ TUCK SUPPORT

Intermediate B Sit in a tuck position (feet slid toward the buttocks) with the hands on the floor by the hips. Lift to a support by extending the arms and attempting to lift the buttocks and feet off the floor.

➤ HALF L-SUPPORT

Intermediate B Perform the tuck support, and then attempt to slowly extend one leg into a pike position, keeping the other leg in a tuck position. Repeat the activity using the other leg.

➤ L-SUPPORT

Advanced Sit in an open pike position (legs straight out in front) with the hands on the floor by the hips. Extend the arms to lift the buttocks and legs off the floor in the open pike position while trying to maintain a vertical position of the torso.

Inverted Balances

In an inverted position, the lower body is above the upper body and head. The following skills are forms of inverted balances. Gymnasts should try to hold each balance for two to three seconds.

➤ TRIPOD

Intermediate A   From a squat position, form a triangle with the hands and head (the head is at the top of the triangle; the head touches the floor at the hairline). Place one knee on each elbow, and lift the hips to balance on the hands and forehead.

➤ DOUBLE-KNEE UPRISE

Intermediate A   From a tripod position, slowly lift the legs to a tuck position and hold. The majority of the body weight should be supported on the hands.

➤ HEADSTAND

Intermediate A   Balance in a tripod, and then extend both the hips and legs to balance in an extended headstand. Support and balance are provided by the arms. The body is extended, showing control and balance.

➤ HEADSTAND ROLL-OUT

Intermediate B Balance in a headstand position. After balancing, allow the legs to lean slightly forward, push with the hands to lift the head slightly off the floor, tuck the head, and roll forward through a squat position to stand.

➤ LEVER

Intermediate B From a stand with arms high, step forward, moving through a lunge. Place the hands on the floor, and lift the back leg as high as possible while keeping the support leg on the floor. Lift the hands from the floor back to a lunge position.

➤ SINGLE-LEG UPRISE TOWARD HANDSTAND

Intermediate B From a stand with arms high, step forward, moving through a lunge. Place the hands on the floor, and lift the back leg as high as possible. Keep the arms extended. Push off the base leg so both feet are in the air (legs do not need to come together in the air). Lower the base leg first, and push off the hands back to a lunge position.

➤ THREE-QUARTER HANDSTAND, SWITCH LEGS

Intermediate B From a stand with arms high, step forward, moving through a lunge. Place the hands on the floor, and lift the back leg as high as possible. Keep the arms extended. Push off the base leg, and switch leg positions in the air, lowering the first leg. Push off the hands back to a lunge position.

➤ WALK THE WALL

Advanced From a prone position with feet against the wall, walk the feet partway up the wall while simultaneously moving the hands closer to the wall. Then slowly reverse the process to return to a prone position. *Coach's note:* Strength will determine how far up the wall the gymnast can go.

➤ HANDSTAND

Advanced From a stand with arms high, step forward to pass through a lunge. Lift the back leg while placing the hands on the floor shoulder-width apart, and push off the front leg. Bring the legs together in a straight handstand position. The head is neutral. Hold momentary balance. Step down and raise the chest to finish in a lunge. *Coach's note:* Spotting is recommended. Assist by lifting the hips and, if necessary, steadying the legs when the gymnast kicks to handstand. Instruct the gymnast to tighten the muscles. Never hold the gymnast by the ankles.

➤ HANDSTAND ROLL FROM WALL

Advanced   Walk the feet up the wall to a hollow handstand position, with the abdomen facing the wall. Push off the wall with the feet, tuck the head, and roll forward on the back to a stand. Arms remain as straight as possible and the shoulder angle is extended to begin the roll. The head should not bear any weight on the roll. Show control and balance. *Coach's note:* An additional mat or skill cushion can be used, and spotting is recommended on the first few attempts.

➤ BRIDGE OVER HIGH EDGE

Advanced   Lie in a supine position with the head toward the high edge of an incline (wedge) mat. Reach the hands overhead. Place the hands on the floor with fingertips pointing toward the mat and as close to the edge of the wedge as possible. Bridge up to support. Show strong, straight arms and extension through the shoulders and upper back in the bridge position (there should be little to no arch in the lower back). With the chest stretching over the fingertips, push off with one leg while lifting the other leg overhead (walkover position), and step down to the floor. *Coach's note:* Spotting is recommended. Assist by lifting the gymnast's hips. Be sure the gymnast is strong enough to support herself in the bridge position.

Springs and Landings

Springs (takeoffs) and landings are two of the most important movements in gymnastics. Virtually every skill requires one or both of these movements. Proper springs and landings can help with skill technique and completion as well as injury prevention and safety. The basic skills presented in this section will help gymnasts learn how to spring and land properly. Chapter 7 covers the basics of safe landings and recovery rolls. These are important skills to teach the gymnasts from the beginning of their time in a gymnastics class. Reinforcement should occur with each lesson. Springs and landings are typically learned during both the basic and intermediate stages of gymnastics.

SPRINGS AND LANDINGS

Jumping From and Landing on Two Feet

These springs and landings involve taking off from two feet, or landing on two feet, or both.

➤ STRETCH JUMP

Basic From a stand on two feet with heels on the floor, bend the knees slightly (demi-plié), arms at the sides. Simultaneously push off the floor by extending through the hips, knees, ankles, and toes and raise the arms forward and upward. While in the air, maintain a stretched (straight) body, with arms by the ears and legs straight and together. Land on two feet, bending the knees slightly and lowering the arms to front middle (safe landing position, as described on page 94 in chapter 7).

➤ TUCK JUMP

Basic Begin as for a stretch jump. As soon as the feet leave the floor, bend both knees forward and upward to a minimum 90-degree hip and knee angle. Before landing, extend the hips and legs to a stretched position. Land in a safe landing position with the arms in front middle position.

➤ SPLIT JUMP

Basic   Begin as for a stretch jump. As soon as the feet leave the floor, separate the legs into a stride split position to a minimum of 30 degrees. Before landing, bring the legs together. Land on two feet in a safe landing position. Arms can be raised or at side middle during the jump.

➤ STRADDLE JUMP

Intermediate A   Begin as for a stretch jump. As soon as the feet leave the floor, separate the legs to a straddle position (right leg extended to the right and left leg extended to the left). Before landing, bring the legs together. Land on two feet in a safe landing position. Arms can be raised or at front middle during the jump.

➤ BOUNDING

Intermediate A   From a stand on two feet, perform a low stretch jump. Upon landing, with little flexion of the hips, knees, or ankles, quickly push off and jump again. Repeat three to five times. Arms should remain up by the ears. After the final jump, finish in a safe landing position.

➤ COMBINATION JUMPS

Intermediate B   To add variety and difficulty, practice combination jumps by connecting two or three jumps together in a series. Start with the same jump repeated, and then advance to different jumps in a series. For example, a sequence could be tuck jump and pike jump.

Jumping From and Landing on One Foot

These springs and landings involve taking off from one foot, or landing on one foot, or both.

➤ HOPPING

Basic Standing on one leg, perform a low stretch jump and land on the same foot. Repeat several times in succession, and then switch legs. Arms can be in various positions: stretched high, low to the sides, low to the front, or side middle.

➤ ASSEMBLÉ

Intermediate A Lift one leg forward and upward, then push off the other leg and bring both legs together in the air. Finish by landing on both feet in a controlled position. Repeat the activity, beginning with the other leg.

➤ HITCH KICK

Intermediate A   Step forward and push off the back foot while swinging the front leg forward and upward. Switch leg positions in the air, and land on the front leg. Arms can be at side middle or stretched high.

➤ STRIDE LEAP

Intermediate B   From a slow run forward, push off one foot to rise in the air, separate the legs to a stride (straight split) position, and land on the front foot with the knee slightly flexed. Repeat the activity, pushing off the other leg. Arms are in opposition to the legs.

➤ SISSONNE

Intermediate B   Step forward, and move the back foot forward to a position behind the front foot. Jump from both feet, and separate the legs to a stride position. Land on the front leg in a low arabesque. Arms can be stretched high, at side middle, or in opposition. Repeat the move on the other side.

Rotations

Rotations are skills that involve movement around an internal axis. Three types of rotations are possible: vertical rotations, horizontal rotations, and anterior–posterior rotations. Rotations can be practiced at all levels, from beginning to advanced.

Vertical Rotations

Vertical rotations are movements around the vertical axis running from head to toe.

➤ PIVOT TURN

Basic   Step forward on relevé with the right foot and then quickly close the left foot behind the right, maintaining the relevé position. Turn quickly to the left 180 degrees in the relevé position. Lower the heels to the floor. Arms can be on the hips or in crown position (curved overhead).

➤ TURN (PIROUETTE)

Basic Step forward, quickly rising up on the ball of the front foot, and turn 90 degrees, 180 degrees, or 360 degrees to finish in various positions. Typically, a turn is performed with the arms raised in a crown position and the big toe of the free leg touching the knee of the support leg; however, arm and free-leg positions can vary.

➤ LOG ROLL

Basic Using an incline (wedge) mat, begin in a supine position on the upper end of the wedge, with the body fully extended. Roll over into a prone position, and continue rolling to the end of the wedge. Repeat the activity, rolling back up the wedge and then rolling in the opposite direction. Log rolls can also be performed on the floor.

➤ STRETCH JUMP WITH TWIST

Intermediate A   Jump up from the floor with the body in an extended (stretched) position, twist 180 degrees or 360 degrees, and land on both feet. Repeat the jump, turning in the opposite direction. Arms should be either stretched straight above the head or in a softer crown position.

Horizontal Rotations

Horizontal rotations are movements around the horizontal axis running from one side of the waist to the other.

Forward Rolling

Horizontal rotations in a forward direction produce forward rolls.

➤ SLIDE OFF INCLINE, FORWARD ROLL

Basic   Begin in a prone position, with the head toward the high end of the wedge; slide forward, placing the hands on the floor next to the wedge. With support on the arms, look at the belly and roll over forward off the wedge and onto the floor. Hands should be placed as close to the edge of the wedge as possible. Arms should be straight and reaching at an angle forward and up at the end of the skill.

119

➤ TIP OVER INCLINE, FORWARD ROLL

Basic   Begin on the shins, positioned on the high end of the wedge facing away from the down slope. Arms are extended high. Reach for the floor with the hands, look at the belly, and roll over forward to finish in a standing position on the floor. Hands should be placed as close to the edge of the wedge as possible. Arms should be as straight as possible and reaching forward and up at an angle at the end of the skill. *Coach's note:* Spotting is recommended. Assist by lifting the hips.

➤ STRADDLE FORWARD ROLL DOWN INCLINE

Intermediate A   Stand on the high edge of the wedge in a straddle position, facing down the wedge. Reach between and behind the legs, and place the hands on the mat to perform a forward roll to stand with feet together. Arms reach forward and up at the end of the skill. Place the upper back on the wedge at the beginning of the roll. The roll can also be done to straddle stand.

➤ TUCK FORWARD ROLL DOWN INCLINE

Intermediate A   From a standing position, squat down on the high end of the wedge, facing down the wedge. Place the hands on the wedge in front of the feet, shoulder-width apart. Raise the hips, tuck the head, and push off the feet to perform a tuck forward roll down the wedge, finishing in a straight stand. Arms are stretched up by the ears or slightly forward at the end of the skill. Maintain the tuck position throughout the roll, and stand up without using the hands to push on the mat.

➤ ROLL UP AND OVER INCLINE

Intermediate A   Step onto the low end of the wedge, facing the up slope. Moving through a scale position (page 105), roll over forward up the wedge to a sitting position on the high edge of the wedge, with arms forward. *Coach's note:* A jump can be added to the end of this skill.

COACHING TIP   On forward rolls, a gymnast's head should be tucked so that the chin is to the chest, the back is rounded, and the back of the head and shoulders are on the mat. The head should not bear weight.

➤ ROLL OVER AND DOWN INCLINE

Intermediate A Facing the high end of the wedge, place the hands on the mat. Jump off both feet to a forward roll down the wedge, finishing in a stand. Arms are stretched up by the ears at the end of the skill. Control is important throughout this skill. *Coach's note:* A spotter may be used if needed.

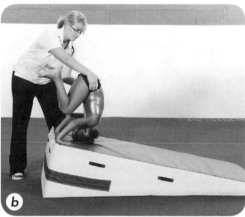

➤ FORWARD ROLL

Intermediate B From a stand, squat down to place the hands on the floor, tuck the head, and perform a forward roll. The back should roll on the floor smoothly from neck to buttocks. Finish in a squat position, and immediately extend the legs to stand. The roll can also be finished in a walkout by keeping one leg tucked while the other leg extends forward slightly as the body rolls along the back. Again, finish by rising to a stand. Arms are stretched upward near the ears at the end of the skill.

➤ STRADDLE FORWARD ROLL

Intermediate B   From a straddle stand, pike and place the hands on the floor slightly in front of the feet. Roll over forward, maintaining a straddle position, and push on the floor between the legs to rise to a straight-leg straddle stand. Arms can be in front, slightly to the sides, or stretched upward at the finish.

➤ PIKE TUCK FORWARD ROLL

Intermediate B   From a stretched standing position with legs together and arms stretched up next to the ears, pike forward at the hips to place the hands on the floor in front of the feet. Round the back and tuck the head to roll over forward. Tuck the body when the hips touch the floor. Finish in a stand with the arms stretched overhead.

➤ HALF HANDSTAND FORWARD ROLL

Advanced   From a stretched standing position with your arms stretched overhead or outward, move through a scale (left or right foot), simultaneously place the hands on the floor, and roll forward, finishing in a stand. Arms are stretched overhead at the finish. The support leg remains in contact with the floor until the back touches on the forward roll.

➤ HANDSTAND FORWARD ROLL OVER AND DOWN INCLINE

Advanced Place the hands on the floor by the high end of the wedge. Push off the feet into a handstand, keeping the arms extended, and lean forward onto the wedge to perform a forward roll over the high edge and down the slope. Finish in a stretched standing position with the arms stretched overhead. *Coach's note:* Spotting is recommended. Assist by holding the gymnast's legs or hips.

➤ HANDSTAND FORWARD ROLL

Advanced Lunge forward, bend at the hips, and place the hands on the floor. Push up through a handstand position, tuck the head, and lower the upper back and shoulders. Roll forward to finish in a stand with the arms stretched overhead. *Coach's note:* Spotting is recommended. Assist by holding the legs or hips as the gymnast kicks up to handstand. Guide the gymnast gently downward into the forward roll.

Backward Rolling

Horizontal rotations in a backward direction produce backward rolls.

➤ ROCKING

Basic From a tuck sit, roll backward until the shoulders touch the floor and the buttocks is raised off the floor, maintaining a tuck position. Practice placing the hands on the floor by the shoulders, with palms down and fingers pointing toward the body. Roll back to the start position.

➤ CANDLESTICK

Basic From a stand, bend the knees to arrive in a tuck sit. Continue rolling backward, and extend the body into a shoulder balance (candlestick), with weight high on the shoulders, toes pointed up, and hip angle as straight as possible. Arms should be straight, with palms on the floor in front of the buttocks.

➤ BACK ROLL DOWN INCLINE

Intermediate A Sit on the high end of the wedge facing away from the down slope. Roll backward with the hands beside the head. Hold the legs in a tuck position, using the hands for support as the body becomes inverted. Finish by pushing off the hands to land on the feet in a tuck position and then extending the legs to stand. Arms can be stretched upward or forward. *Coach's note:* This skill can also be performed starting from a stand on the wedge.

➤ BACK STRADDLE ROLL DOWN INCLINE

Intermediate A Sit on the high end of the wedge facing away from the down slope. Roll backward, separating the legs, with the hands beside the head. Straighten the legs to a straddle position, using the hands for support. Finish by pushing off the hands to a straddle stand. *Coach's note: This skill can also be performed from a stand on the wedge.*

➤ BACK ROLL DOWN INCLINE TO STRETCH JUMP

Intermediate A Perform a back roll down the wedge to a stand. Concentrate on rolling in a straight line. As the legs are extending to the standing position, jump upward with arms stretched overhead and land on the mat on two feet showing control. *Coach's note: This skill can also be performed from a stand on the wedge.*

COACHING TIP For backward rolls, a gymnast's head should be tucked with chin to chest. Proper hand placement includes hands beside the head with fingers pointing toward the shoulders. The gymnast uses the arms to push as the hips roll over the head. This helps take the weight off the head and neck to complete the roll.

➤ STRADDLE TUCK BACKWARD ROLL

Intermediate B   From a straddle stand, roll backward while simultaneously reaching between the legs for assistance. Continue rolling backward, using the arms to support the body, and bring the knees together. Finish in a squat stand with the arms to the sides or straight out in front of the body.

➤ STRADDLE BACKWARD ROLL

Intermediate B   From a straddle position, either standing or sitting, roll backward while maintaining a straddle position. Push off the hands, finishing in a straddle stand with the arms stretched upward by the ears.

➤ BACKWARD ROLL

Intermediate B   From a stretched standing position, perform a backward roll to a stretched standing position with the arms stretched straight up by the ears.

➤ PIKE TUCK BACKWARD ROLL

Intermediate B Begin in a pike standing position, bend forward, and reach backward to catch the body's weight with the hands as the roll is initiated. As the buttocks touches the floor, continue to roll backward by tucking the knees and the arms up beside the head. Push

off the hands, moving through a squat position and finishing in a stand with the arms stretched upward. *Coach's note:* Spotting is recommended. Lift the gymnast at the hips when assisting.

➤ TUCK PIKE BACKWARD ROLL

Intermediate B From a squat position, roll backward and straighten the legs to finish in a pike to stand with the arms stretched upward at the end of the skill.

➤ BACKWARD ROLL WITH JUMPS

Intermediate B   Perform jumps in various positions before and after a backward roll. Show balance before rolling backward, support on the hands during the roll, and control during the final jump and landing. Arms are stretched upward at the completion of the skills.

➤ BACKWARD ROLL WITH STRAIGHT ARMS TO PIKE STAND

Advanced From a squat position, roll backward. Maintaining straight arms and an inward-facing hand position, reach backward so that the sides of the little fingers contact the floor first behind the head. As the hips roll backward through vertical, press down against the floor with arms as straight as possible. Extend the legs into a pike position to finish in a straight stand with arms stretched overhead.

➤ BACKWARD ROLL TO FRONT SUPPORT

Advanced Perform a backward roll with straight arms. As the hips are rolling over the head, extend the legs to a hollow body position, and maintain this position to finish in a push-up position (front support) with legs together and balls of the feet on the floor.

➤ LOW BACK EXTENSION

Advanced Sit on the high end of the wedge. Roll backward down the wedge, placing the hands by the shoulders. Extend at the hips and knees as the hands contact the wedge, and extend the arms to lift the shoulders off the wedge. Finish by stepping down one leg at a time to a lunge and extending the arms overhead. *Coach's note:* Spotting is recommended. Lift the gymnast at the legs or hips when assisting.

Anterior–Posterior Rotations

Anterior–posterior rotations are movements around the anterior–posterior axis running from the front to the back of the body.

➤ HAND-HAND-FOOT-FOOT

Intermediate A Begin standing in a straddle position on a half circle of rope, facing the center of the half circle. Perform a cartwheel-type movement around the rope by moving sideward, hand-hand-foot-foot (cartwheel action), finishing in a straddle standing position. Arms are stretched straight overhead at the completion. Repeat the activity in the opposite direction. *Coach's note:* Adjust the size of the half circle to the child.

➤ HALF CARTWHEEL OVER MATS

Intermediate A From a straddle stand perpendicular to a folded panel mat, place the hands on the mat using a cartwheel action to move to the other side of the mat. Arms are stretched upward and slightly outward at the completion. Repeat the activity with the other foot first.

➤ LOW CARTWHEEL OVER ROPE

Intermediate A Reach out and over a rope (12 to 24 inches [30 to 60 cm] high), placing the hands on a mat, and push off one leg at a time using the cartwheel action to finish in a straddle stand on the other side of the rope. Arms are stretched upward at the completion. Repeat the activity on the other side.

COACHING TIP A small octagon mat or foam block could be used in place of the rope when teaching a cartwheel.

➤ CARTWHEEL

Intermediate B From a straddle stand with arms stretched outward, perform a cartwheel. Finish the cartwheel in a side stand, and progress to a lunge. Arms are stretched upward at the completion. Repeat the activity on both sides. *Coach's note:* Spotting is recommended on the first few attempts. Assist the gymnast by lifting at the hips.

➤ THREE STEPS TO CARTWHEEL

Intermediate B   Take three walking steps, raising the arms during the third step, and perform a cartwheel. Finish the cartwheel in a side stand, and progress to a lunge. Arms are stretched upward and slightly outward at the completion. Repeat on the other side.

COACHING TIP   Things to look for in the performance of a cartwheel include head neutral, with eyes focused on hands; legs and hips extended (a good straddle throughout); and control and balance from start to finish.

➤ POWER HURDLE CARTWHEEL

Advanced   Jump from two feet, stretching tall. Come down on one foot, with the other foot reaching forward in a lunge position. Arms should be up by the ears, and the body should be leaning slightly forward. Pass through the lunge position to perform a cartwheel. Arms are stretched upward and slightly outward at the completion.

➤ CARTWHEEL-STYLE ROUND-OFF

Advanced Step forward to place the hands on the floor and perform a cartwheel. As the first leg contacts the floor, turn the body 90 degrees to face the starting point, and close the second leg to the first to finish with feet together in a stand. Arms are stretched overhead at the completion.

➤ STEP INTO ROUND-OFF

Advanced Step forward through a lunge with a strong push off the front leg. Place the hands on the floor. As the feet pass overhead (through vertical), push off the hands, turn 90 degrees, and close the legs together quickly, just before the first foot contacts the floor. Finish with the knees slightly flexed and, if possible, the body leaning backward. Arms are stretched overhead at the completion.

Vault Skills

9

At the beginner level, vault skills can be learned and practiced using folded panel mats, trapezoid mats, or spotting blocks in place of the vault table. This allows for lower, softer, and safer equipment and progressions for the athletes. Additionally, for younger children, smaller vaulting boards may be more appropriate.

As a lead-up to vault drills and skills, gymnasts should be proficient at running, hurdling, jumping, and landing. Reinforce these basics with every lesson. Even when your gymnasts have mastered these progressions, it is helpful to use them as a warm-up for more advanced vault training sessions.

Running

These more basic drills help gymnasts learn running technique, develop power and speed, use their arms correctly, and feel comfortable running down the runway toward the vault.

RUNNING

➤ 40-FOOT RUN

Basic Run down a vault runway or flat, open surface for approximately 40 feet (12 m). Vary speed with each run, moving from slow to medium to fast.

COACHING TIP Proper running technique includes lifting the heels toward the buttocks, raising the front knee so that the thigh is horizontal, leaning slightly forward, and focusing the eyes on the end of the runway. The arms should be bent approximately 90 degrees, should pump forward and backward with each stride, and should remain close to the sides.

➤ HIGH KNEES

Intermediate A Run with shorter strides and an upright torso (little to no forward lean), raising the thighs to horizontal or above with each step.

➤ REAR KICKS

Intermediate A Run with shorter strides and an upright torso (little to no forward lean), bending the knees to full flexion, with the heels coming up toward the buttocks.

➤ DEER LEAPS

Intermediate B Run with extra-long strides.

➤ ONE-LEG RUN

Intermediate B   Perform a hopping motion on one leg, using the arms and the free leg to generate additional speed and power. Repeat on the other leg.

COACHING TIP   One way to help athletes with the one-leg run is to time them. They can work toward their personal-best speed on each leg. As the athletes push to go faster, they will naturally use their free leg and arms to generate additional speed and power.

Hurdling

Hurdling is the act of transitioning from the run into a jump on the vaulting board in preparation for performing the skill. These basic and intermediate drills help gymnasts become more proficient at this transition and practice proper technique.

HURDLING

➤ JUMP ON TARGET

Basic   Take one step, lift one leg forward and upward, push off the other leg, and bring both legs together in the air. Land with feet together in the hoop (on target). Body should be upright, with knees flexed slightly and in front of shoul-ders. Arms remain in front middle position or can be stretched upward.

➤ ARM CIRCLE

Basic Standing in place, practice the underarm swing used with the hurdle. Move arms in a small, quick circle from the sides through backward low position to finish in front. Repeat.

➤ HURDLE ON TARGET

Basic Take one step, lift one leg forward and upward, push off the other leg, and bring both legs together in the air. Simultaneously circle the arms backward. Finish by landing on both feet in the hoop (on target), with the arms at front middle position. *Coach's note:* After landing on target, gymnasts can progress to an immediate rebound (spring upward with the arms stretched upward).

COACHING TIP During a hurdle, arm coordination is important. The hurdle should be long and low to maintain forward momentum; at this point, the arms circle backward. The back leg quickly joins the front leg, and the body is nearly vertical when contacting the board (the shoulders should be slightly behind the feet and the arms stretched slightly backward).

➤ RUN, HURDLE, REBOUND, STRETCH JUMP

Intermediate A   From a short run (seven to nine steps), perform a hurdle onto the springboard, rebound, and perform a stretch jump to a controlled landing position on the mat. Arms are at front middle on landing. *Coach's note:* At least an 8-inch (20 cm) mat is recommended for landing.

➤ RUN, HURDLE, REBOUND

Intermediate A Make the previous drill more difficult by replacing the stretch jump with other types of jumps such as a tuck jump, straddle jump, stretch jump with 180-degree turn, and so on.

Jumping

Practicing jumps can help gymnasts learn how to use their arms and legs together, land and rebound properly, and develop greater power. Unless otherwise noted, these drills use stacked panel mats approximately 24 inches (60 cm) high, positioned perpendicular to the direction of motion. The vaulting board is then placed close to the front mat.

JUMPING

➤ TRAVELING JUMPS UP AND DOWN

Intermediate A   Travel forward on a mat (folded panel or otherwise) with support on the hands by jumping from the side of the mat to the top of the mat, to the other side of the mat, back to the top, and so forth. Each time the feet have support on the floor, move the hands forward 6 to 12 inches (15 to 30 cm).

➤ JUMP-JUMP-STRETCH JUMP

Intermediate A   Run, hurdle, and rebound off the board, landing on the first folded panel mat. Then jump from the first mat to the second mat, and jump off the second mat showing a stretched position. Execute a safe landing position (knees slightly bent, torso hollowed, arms at front middle). Maintain balance and control throughout the drill, keeping the legs together.

➤ TRAVELING JUMPS OVER AND BACK

Intermediate B   Travel forward on a mat (folded panel or otherwise) with support on the hands by jumping from one side of the mat to the other without touching the feet on the top of the mat, raising the arms for each landing.

➤ JUMP-JUMP SERIES

Intermediate B   Using the technique for the jump-jump-stretch jump (page 143), make the drill progressively more difficult by replacing the final jump with other types of jumps such as a tuck jump, straddle jump, pike jump, stretch jump with 180-degree turn, and so on.

➤ TRIPLE JUMP TO FORWARD ROLL

Intermediate B   Run, hurdle, and rebound off the board, landing on the first mat. Then jump from the first mat to the second mat, jump off the second mat showing a stretched position, and land on the feet in demi-plié with a slight forward body lean. Reach forward, tuck the head, and do a forward roll to stand. Finish in a stretched standing position with arms overhead. Jumps should be done with good balance and control.

Landing

Learning to land in the safe landing position is very important in gymnastics. Gymnasts need to feel comfortable jumping from various heights and landing in the safe landing position naturally and automatically.

LANDING

➤ STRETCH JUMP AND STICK

Intermediate A From a stand on the vault surface (mat stack or vault table), perform a stretch jump to a safe landing position. Stick the safe landing position with arms at front middle. Reinforce holding the stuck landing position for two or three seconds. *Coach's note:* The vault surface should not be higher than the gymnast's chest height.

COACHING TIP On all jumping and landing skills, reinforce correct technique, including a controlled landing. A controlled landing means the athlete can and should hold the safe landing position for a couple of seconds before walking off the mat. Tell the athlete, "Stick it!"

Squat Vaults

The squat vault is the gymnast's first experience going over the vaulting table. This section includes developmental drills that will provide gymnasts with the skills necessary to be able to vault.

SQUAT VAULTS

➤ SQUAT JUMPS IN A SERIES

Basic   From a squat position on the floor, lean forward and push off the legs while reaching forward with the hands. With momentary support on the hands, bring the knees forward to return to a squat position. Repeat for a series of three to five jumps.

➤ SQUAT THRUSTS IN A SERIES

Basic   From a front support position on the floor, shift the weight to the hands, and bring the knees forward to a squat position. Then return to a front support. Repeat the activity three to five times.

➤ SQUAT ON, BOUNCE, SQUAT ON

Intermediate A From a squat position on top of a stack of mats, shift the weight onto the hands, extend the legs backward, and snap the legs down to the board, keeping the hands on the stacked mats during the foot contact with the board. Rebound off the board, and return to a squat position on the mats.

➤ SQUAT ON, FORWARD ROLL

Intermediate A With the springboard close to a stack of mats, stand on the springboard with the hands on the mat stack and bounce from the board, raising the hips to a squat position on top of the mats. Forward roll on top of the stacked mats to a stand on the mats. *Optional:* After the forward roll, perform a stretch jump from the mats to the floor with a controlled landing.

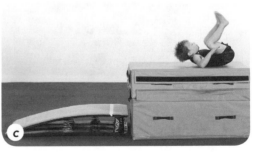

➤ BOUNCE, SQUAT ON, JUMP OFF

Intermediate A From a stand on the springboard with the hands on top of a stack of mats, bounce from the board to a squat on the mats. Immediately jump forward off the mats with a controlled landing.

➤ SQUAT ON, JUMP OFF

Intermediate B Walk (or run) forward three to five steps, hurdle, and rebound off the board with two feet. Vault to a squat position on the mats and immediately jump forward off the mats with a controlled landing.

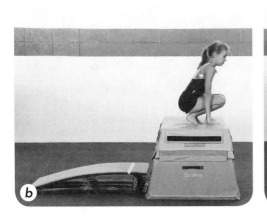

➤ SQUAT VAULT

Intermediate B Run three to five steps, hurdle, and rebound off the springboard with two feet. Using an underarm lift, reach forward with the arms to a front support, with the legs extended to the back and the hips slightly above the shoulders. Simultaneously push off the mats with both hands and tuck the knees. The shoulders rise with the push from the mats, and the head and torso are vertical as the body passes over the mats. Extend the legs to land in a controlled position.

Prehandspring Vaults

These are important drills and progressions leading up to a handspring vault. It is highly recommended that the coach take the gymnast through the proper drills and progressions as stated in this section. Once the gymnast has acquired the basics, she will be ready to begin the next phase of a handspring vault.

PREHANDSPRING VAULTS

➤ DONKEY KICKS

Intermediate A   While standing on the board, place the hands on the stacked mats and bounce on the board, driving the heels back and up into the air toward a handstand position. Upon landing, immediately spring back up. Repeat numerous times, keeping the head neutral and working to achieve a straight, slightly hollow body shape. This drill can be done in the tuck position, with progression to a pike, and then finally with straight legs. *Coach's note:* Spotting is recommended on the first few attempts. Assist the gymnast by holding her at the hips.

➤ HANDSTAND FALL TO BACK

Intermediate B Move through a lunge position to kick up to a handstand on the springboard. Pass through vertical and land flat on the back on a skill cushion (at least 8 inches [20 cm]). Maintain a straight, tight body with the head in neutral position throughout.

➤ HANDSTAND HOPS

Intermediate B Passing through a lunge position, swing the arms from backward low to forward high, place the hands on the floor, and kick up to a handstand. Keeping the arms straight, extend the shoulders quickly, creating a push (block) off the floor to perform small hops on the hands. Keep the body straight and tight, with legs together. Step down to a lunge position. *Coach's note:* Spotting is recommended.

➤ HANDSTAND BLOCK TO BACK

Advanced   Take one to three steps, swing the arms from backward low to forward middle, place the hands on the springboard while moving through a lunge, and kick up to a handstand. The arms remain straight, and the shoulders extend quickly so that the hands block off the board. Show flight through vertical, with the body rotating to land in a straight hollow lying position on the back on a skill cushion (at least 16 inches [40 cm]). The head is neutral throughout, the body is tight, and the legs are together.

➤ DIVE FORWARD ROLL ONTO MATS

Advanced   From a short run (seven to nine steps), hurdle onto the board and rebound, extending the legs and reaching forward to place the hands on the mats. Maintain a hollow body position while lifting the hips over the shoulders and head. Upon contact with the mats, bend the arms slightly, tuck the chin, and perform a tucked forward roll onto the mats. *Coach's note:* The mat stack should be waist height for the gymnast, including a skill cushion on top.

10

Bar Skills

For beginner gymnasts, a lower bar rail, at approximately the athlete's chest height, should be used. If the rail will not adjust lower, you can build up the mats underneath the bar. For the skills presented in this section, a single bar rail or the low bar of an uneven bars apparatus is most appropriate.

Athletes should be proficient at swings, another dominant movement pattern, before beginning intermediate and more advanced skills on bars. Part of learning how to swing includes gripping the bar, hanging, and practicing small swings. These basics are covered in this chapter along with support, casting, circling, and dismount skills.

Grips

The grip is the position of the hands on the bar. A proper grip allows the gymnast to hang and swing efficiently.

GRIPS

➤ OVERGRIP

Basic   Place the palms of both hands on the bar, with the fingers facing away from the body. The hands should wrap around the top of the bar.

➤ UNDERGRIP

Basic   Place the palms of both hands on the bar, with the fingers facing toward the body. The hands should wrap underneath the bar.

➤ MIXED GRIP

Basic Place both hands on the bar, one in overgrip and one in undergrip.

Hanging

Hanging is the act of grasping the bar while suspended below it in various positions. One must show the ability to hang and hold onto a bar before she can progress to any other activity on bars.

➤ LONG HANG

Basic With hands in overgrip, hang with a straight body from the bar. Feet should be off the mat. The long hang can be adapted in order to use a lower bar rail. The gymnast can bend his legs behind him at a 90-degree angle to avoid hitting his feet on the mat. *Coach's note:* Assist the gymnast with the release and landing on the mat if he cannot reach the mat on his own.

➤ FLEXED ARM HANG

Intermediate A From a long-hang position with hands in overgrip, flex the arms to raise the chin slightly above the bar. Hold this position for five seconds. Legs should remain straight and together.

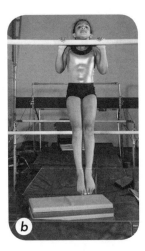

Swings and Glides

Swinging is a fundamental movement on bars. Swinging involves grasping the bar and swinging back and forth underneath it. Hand grip may need to be adjusted at the top of the backswing so the gymnast maintains a consistent grasp on the bar. Generally, a swing from back to front with the feet leading the body, such as before a kip (a move from below the bar to above it) or other similar skill, is referred to as a glide. Swings and glides are typically beginner- to intermediate-level skills; the gymnast must begin with swings and glides as a lead-up to more advanced bar skills.

SWINGS AND GLIDES

➤ TUCK SWING

Basic From a standing position with arms extended and hands in overgrip, swing under the bar in a tuck position and back to the starting point. Place feet on the mat to stop the swing, and then release the bar.

➤ RUN-THROUGH HALF TURN

Intermediate A   From a stand with extended arms and hands in overgrip on the bar, run under the bar, stop and release the bar, do a 180-degree turn, regrip with overgrip, and run through the bar again.

➤ RUN-THROUGH HALF TURN SWING

Intermediate A   From a stand with extended arms and hands in overgrip, run under the bar, stop and release the bar, do a 180-degree turn, regrip with overgrip, and swing under in a tuck position. The gymnast can then release the bar to finish in a stand, or she can continue to hold onto the bar until she swings back under it before releasing to finish in a stand.

➤ STRADDLE AND PIKE GLIDES

Intermediate B   From a stand on the mat, jump from both feet, lifting the hips backward and upward to grasp the bar in overgrip with hands shoulder-width apart. Swing the body forward, with the feet leading, in pike or straddle position. Extend the body at the completion of the forward glide swing. Swing backward, maintaining straight legs. At the completion of the backward swing, the feet contact the mat to end in a straight stand.

COACHING TIP   To generate greater speed in their glides, tell your gymnasts to concentrate on raising their hips after they jump from the mat to grasp the bar.

➤ SWING HALF TURN

Intermediate B   From a standing position with arms extended and hands in overgrip, swing under the bar in a tuck position. As the body reaches the peak of the front swing, initiate the turn by turning the hips and shoulders. Release one hand, and reach to the other side of the hand still on the bar. Quickly release the second hand to change from mixed grip to overgrip. Regrasp the bar. Swing through underneath the bar.

Supports

Supports are positions in which the gymnast's weight is supported by the bar. Typically the gymnast's torso is at bar height or above, and the legs may be extended below the bar. This a fundamental starting position for many skills such as circles and casts.

SUPPORTS

➤ FRONT SUPPORT

Basic This is a preparatory position with support on the bar. The arms are as straight as possible, the upper thighs or hips rest on the bar, and the legs are straight and extend downward. Feet are elevated off the mat.

➤ SINGLE-LEG CUT TO SUPPORT

Intermediate A From a front support, shift weight to one arm while leaning to that side, and lift the opposite leg over the bar. Release the non-weight-bearing hand as the leg swings over the bar. Finish in stride support (one leg over the bar and the other in back of the bar) with overgrip hand placement.

Casting

A cast is a preparatory movement to gain momentum and speed for the skill that follows, such as a hip circle (a basic skill). A true cast is done from a support position to a handstand; however, beginner gymnasts may practice casting to horizontal as they are learning the skill.

CASTING

➤ CAST

Intermediate A   From a front support, with shoulders slightly in front of the bar, swing the legs forward and then backward and upward to horizontal. Push down on the bar, and extend through the shoulders to rise off the bar; shoulders remain slightly in front of the bar. Return to the bar in front support position. Keep arms straight, keep legs straight and together, and lower to support with control.

➤ CAST DISMOUNT

Intermediate A   Perform a cast. As the body reaches the maximum height in the cast, push away and release the bar. Maintain a tight hollow body position in flight, and land in a controlled position on the mat.

Circling

Because they are the building basics for more difficult bar skills, circling skills are important ones to master. Circling skills are learned at the intermediate and advanced levels in gymnastics.

Circling Backward

Backward circles on bars include skills such as pullovers and back hip circles. A pullover is a basic mount on bars and an important training skill. Pullovers are a safe way for gymnasts to mount or climb onto the bar in order to perform other skills. Training and drills for pullovers help gymnasts develop strength, gripping technique, and rotation awareness with a finish in a support position. A back hip circle is a basic circling skill that is a progression to many more challenging skills.

➤ SKIN THE CAT

Intermediate A   From a stand on the mat, grasp the bar in overgrip. Kick the feet off the mat toward the bar, bringing them together in the air. As the feet come near the bar, stick them under the bar between the hands and arms, and raise the hips up to turn over. Pull the hips through the arms, and slowly lower the feet toward the mat to what's known as a German hang position. To reverse, pull the hips, legs, and feet back through the arms, and lower to the starting position on the mat. *Coach's note:* Spotting is recommended. Assist by holding the gymnast's hips.

COACHING TIP   Especially for beginners, it is recommended that the bar be low enough for the athlete to touch her feet on the mat and support her weight in the German hang position at the end of the skill.

➤ WAIST TO BAR

Intermediate A From a stand, step forward and lift one leg upward, pulling the waist to the bar. Slowly return to the mat.

➤ CANDLESTICK HANG

Intermediate A From a stand, step forward and lift one leg upward, pulling the hips to the bar. Bring the legs together, and hold the inverted position with the hips or upper legs touching the bar. Arms should be extended, and the body should be in a hollow position. Lower slowly to the mat.

COACHING TIP For an easier progression for skills involving hips or waist to bar, have the gymnast start from a stand on a folded mat placed slightly in front of the bar. This raises the gymnast and her hips closer to the bar to start.

➤ KICK TO PULLOVER

Intermediate B From a stand, with hands in overgrip, push off the mat with one leg, and then lift both legs over the bar. Pull the bar toward the waist, rotating the shoulders backward over the bar and shifting the wrists to finish in front support.

➤ BACK HIP PULLOVER

Intermediate B From a stand, with hands in overgrip, jump off two feet, pulling the bar to the waist. Rotate backward over the bar and finish in front support. *Coach's note:* Spotting is recommended.

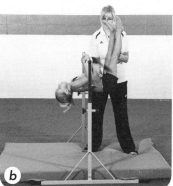

➤ CAST, BACK HIP CIRCLE

Advanced   From a front support, cast away from the bar. As the hips return to the bar, lean the shoulders backward, creating enough momentum to pull the bar toward the waist and rotate backward around the bar. Maintain a hollow body position with straight arms and legs throughout. Head is neutral. Look for continuous motion around the bar to finish in a front support position. *Coach's note:* Spotting is recommended. Stand slightly to the side of the gymnast with arms positioned under the bar. After the gymnast casts, catch the gymnast's legs or hips as she rotates around the bar.

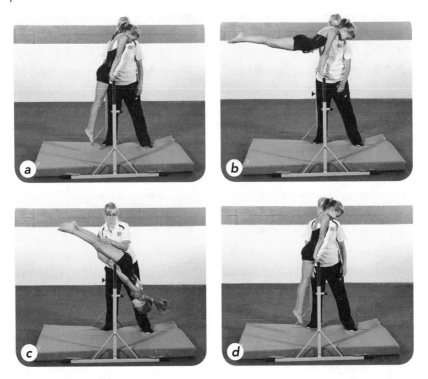

COACHING TIP   Progressions for a back hip circle include a flexed back hip circle (with arms and knees slightly bent, making the body smaller to rotate around the bar) and a piked back hip circle (with flexion at the waist to get the legs around the bar and the hands and chest rotating to the finish position).

Circling Forward

Forward circles help gymnasts gain additional rotational awareness and, most important, learn to shift their hands around the bar. Some forward circles also use undergrip and mixed-grip hand positions to give gymnasts more experience. Gymnasts begin acquiring these skills at the intermediate level and continue to improve them at the advanced level once they have mastered specific body and leg positions.

➤ FORWARD ROLLOVER

Intermediate B   From a controlled front support, with overgrip, undergrip, or mixed grip, roll over the bar forward and slowly lower the body to the mat. Shift the hands forward around the bar, and maintain the grip on the bar until full support on the legs is achieved. Legs can be together or split but should be slightly flexed (do not land with straight legs) when contacting the mat.

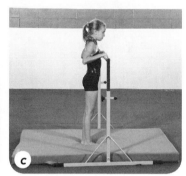

COACHING TIP   For added difficulty in the forward rollover, have the gymnast start by jumping from the mat to front support position and then going immediately into the rollover.

➤ SINGLE-KNEE UPRISE

Intermediate B   From a single-knee hang, extend the nonhanging leg out, down, and back, generating force (pendular body swing) to rotate around the bar forward to finish in a stride support. Arms pull at the peak of the backward swing, and wrists shift to achieve support position. *Coach's note:* Spotting is recommended. Reaching under the bar, hold one wrist and support the gymnast's back as she rotates to the finish position on top of the bar.

➤ ROCK BACK TO SINGLE-KNEE UPRISE

Intermediate B   From a front support, perform a single-leg cut to support, rock back to a single-knee hang, and extend the nonhanging leg out, down, and back, generating force to rotate around the bar to finish in a stride support.

➤ SINGLE-KNEE FORWARD ROLLOVER

Advanced   From a front support, do a single-leg cut to support, and change to an undergrip to roll over the bar forward to a single-knee hang. *Coach's note:* Spotting is recommended. Hold onto one wrist and support the gymnast's back and hips throughout the move.

➤ HALF CIRCLE FORWARD

Advanced   Perform the single-knee forward rollover with both legs extended, finishing in an inverted stride hang. *Coach's note:* Spotting is recommended. Support the gymnast's back and hips throughout the move.

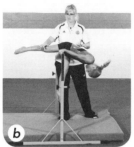

➤ STRIDE CIRCLE

Advanced   From a front support, do a single-leg cut to stride support, and change hands to an undergrip. Lift the body upward off the bar, and lift the cut leg forward, placing the thigh of the back leg against the bar. Lean forward and circle the bar in a stride position to finish in stride support. Arms and legs should remain straight. Extend the upper body, and shift hands to the top of the bar near completion of the circle. *Coach's note:* Spotting is recommended. Stand on the side of the bar next to the gymnast; hold onto one wrist and support the gymnast's back and hips throughout the move.

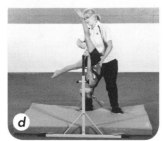

Dismounts

A dismount is the last skill performed by the gymnast in order to leave the bar and land on the ground safely in a standing position. A dismount may be initiated from the high bar or the low bar. All dismounts finish in the safe landing position: knees slightly bent, torso in a slightly hollow shape, and arms at forward middle position. While dismounts are practiced at all levels, gymnasts must master the basics prior to performing a proper and safe dismount.

DISMOUNTS

➤ FLOOR BAR SQUAT-ON

Intermediate A From a push-up position (front support) with hands on a floor bar, jump from the feet, bending the knees and placing the balls of the feet on the bar in a balanced squat position. Immediately jump forward to a controlled landing on the floor.

➤ FLOOR BAR RECOVERY ROLL

Intermediate A Perform a squat on the floor bar, and jump off the bar to land on a mat. Immediately do a shoulder roll forward to stand. Emphasize pulling the arms in toward the body, as with all safety rolls. *Coach's note:* An 8-inch [20 cm] skill cushion is recommended.

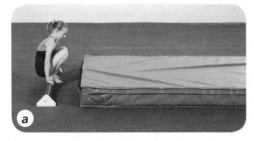
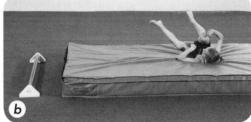

➤ JUMP UNDERSWING, SHOOT TO STAND

Intermediate A From a stand with extended arms and hands in an overgrip position, jump and flex at the waist, bringing the ankles close to the bar (in a pike or straddle position). Hold this position and swing under the bar, extending the body upward and outward. Release the hands, and land on the mat in a controlled landing position.

➤ CLIMB TO STRADDLE UNDERSWING

Intermediate B From a stand with extended arms and hands in an overgrip position, lift one leg, placing that foot on the bar directly outside the hand position. Jump off the other leg, raising the hips and lifting the leg to place it outside the other hand. Arms remain straight. Continue with the underswing, holding this position the entire time. At the end of the underswing, the feet come off the bar first. Then release the hands to land on the mat in a controlled landing position. Feet should remain in contact with the bar until the peak of the upswing.

➤ JUMP TO STRADDLE SOLE CIRCLE DISMOUNT

Intermediate B From a stand with extended arms and hands in an overgrip position, jump to a straddle position, flexing at the waist and placing the feet on the bar outside the hands. Next, initiate the underswing. At the end of the underswing, release the bar (feet and then hands) to land on the mat in a controlled landing position. *Coach's note:* Spotting is recommended.

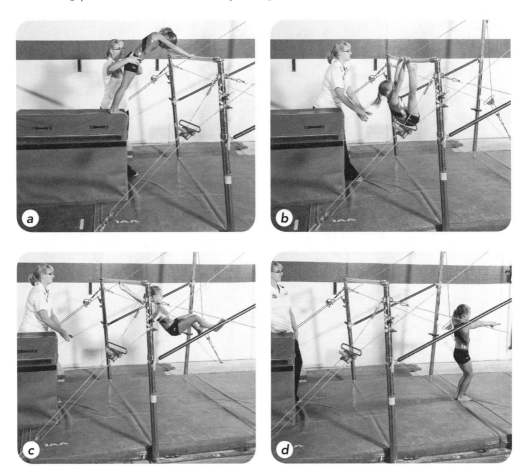

COACHING TIP To gain height on the jump and raise the hips at the start of the underswing, have the athlete jump from stacked mats.

➤ JUMP OFF FORWARD

Intermediate B   From a front support position, bring one foot up on the bar, slide the foot close to the hands, and then move the hands so the foot is between them. Push to stand on both feet, and then jump forward off the bar to land on the mat in a controlled position. *Coach's note:* Spotting is recommended. Assist by holding the hips (while the gymnast is climbing), and then the shoulder and wrist.

➤ CASTS IN TUCK, PIKE, AND STRADDLE

Advanced From a front support, cast hips at shoulder height and tuck; return to bar. Recast showing pike; return to bar. Recast showing straddle; return to bar.

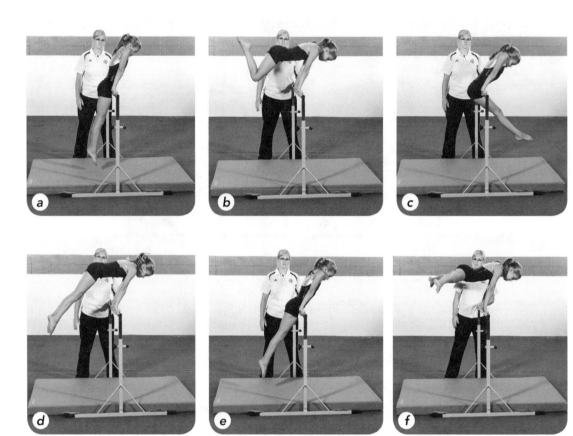

➤ CLIMB TO STRADDLE SOLE CIRCLE DISMOUNT

Advanced From a front support, climb to a straddle stand on the bar, lean backward, underswing, and release the bar (feet and then hands) to land on the mat in a controlled landing position. *Coach's note:* Spotting is recommended.

➤ CAST, SQUAT ON TO PIKE SOLE CIRCLE DISMOUNT

Advanced From a front support, cast with straight legs. Bend the legs to bring the balls of the feet to the bar in a tucked position between the hands. Immediately straighten the arms and legs, and pull the bar against the bottom of the feet. Lean backward to initiate the underswing dismount. Release the bar (feet and then hands), and land in a controlled position on the mat. *Coach's note:* Spotting is recommended.

BEAM

Some of the first things gymnasts should learn when it comes to the balance beam are how to maintain balance on the beam and how to fall and land properly. Your gymnasts must know that it is all right if they fall, and you should teach them the proper landing position—knees slightly bent, chest up, and arms extended forward at heart level. Do not allow the gymnasts to land by placing their hands on the floor. Also, beginner gymnasts need to know how to climb up on the beam to get started or after a fall. Spend time working on these basics before beginning other activities on the balance beam.

Gymnasts should progress through the same dominant movement patterns as presented for floor, including locomotions, statics, springs, rotations, and landings (or dismounts). Gymnasts should be competent in these movements on the floor and on a line on the floor before moving to a low balance beam, where they will also practice beam-specific skills, such as mounts. Gymnasts can then advance to a beam at medium height (no higher than the gymnasts' chest).

COACHING TIP The "freeze" technique is helpful to teach young children how to maintain balance on the beam. When you say "Freeze," the gymnast should stop all movement, bend her knees slightly, and extend her arms in front of herself at chest height (similar to a safe landing position). This automatically teaches the child to keep her center of gravity over her feet (base of support) and the balance beam. You can also test her by gently pushing on her shoulders to see if she can continue to maintain the balanced position. Practice the freeze position on a line on the floor first, and then progress to the beam.

Locomotions

These are similar activities to those discussed for the floor apparatus and include movements that help children develop agility, coordination, balance, and strength and that let them have fun being active.

LOCOMOTIONS

➤ WALK FORWARD AND BACKWARD

Basic Walk forward and backward by placing one foot in front of or behind the other. This can be done on flat feet. Keep the head up and eyes focused toward the end of the beam, and maintain balance and control throughout.

➤ SLIDE STEP SIDEWARD

Basic Facing sideways, slide one foot to the side and close the other foot to it (move the left foot, and then the right). Arms can be out to the sides.

➤ RELEVÉ WALK

Basic Walk forward and backward in relevé (on the balls of the feet). Lower heels at the end of the beam. Arms should be overhead in the crown position or at side middle.

➤ WALK FORWARD AND BACKWARD WITH LEVEL CHANGES

Basic Walk forward two or three steps in relevé and then two or three steps on flat feet. *Coach's note:* Establish a pattern, and have the gymnasts follow that pattern across the beam (e.g., up, up, up, down, down, up, up, up, down, down). Arms are overhead in the crown position or held at side middle.

COACHING TIP At this point, it is important to teach the gymnasts what to do once they reach the end of the balance beam. They must know how to turn around and how to jump down from the beam. Pivot turns and squat turns are fundamental skills to introduce early on.

179

➤ COUPÉ WALK

Intermediate A Step forward onto one foot, and then bring the second foot forward so the toe touches the ankle, with the knee pointing forward. Pause in that position. Extend that foot forward, bring the opposite foot to the ankle, and repeat. Perform first on flat feet, and then in relevé. Arms are held at side middle.

➤ LIFT STEPS FORWARD AND BACKWARD

Intermediate A Stand facing the end of the beam. Walk forward by extending one leg up in front of the body and placing it back on the beam in front of the first foot. Continue down the beam in the same manner. To perform backward, lift the leg up behind the body. Arms can be stretched outward or held at side middle.

COACHING TIP It can also be beneficial for gymnasts to practice running, marching steps, and other locomotions on the balance beam. Be creative when introducing beginner gymnasts to the beam.

➤ SQUAT TO PIKE

Intermediate A From a standing position, squat down and place the hands on the beam in front of the feet, and then extend the legs to a pike position. Return to a squat position, and then extend to stand.

➤ LOW CHASSÉ

Intermediate B Slide the front foot forward on the beam, and push off with the back foot. While in the air, close the back foot behind the front foot, and then land on the back foot (gallop with pointed toes). Arms can be out to the sides or held at side middle.

➤ BEAM WALKING ON ALL FOURS

Intermediate B Walk across the beam with hands and feet on the beam and the body in a tuck position, then pike. This is similar to the bear walk (page 100).

➤ LUNGE SERIES

Intermediate B   Stand in lunge position. Lower to a low lunge, and then place the hands on the beam in front of the flexed leg. Lower to a shin scale, placing one shin on the beam with the other leg extended, and then to a straddle-sit position.

➤ STAND SERIES

Intermediate B   Begin in a straddle-sit position facing the end of the beam. Swing the legs behind the body, and place the feet on top of the beam. Push up and back by extending the arms to come to a squat stand, and then to a stretched stand.

➤ BODY WAVE

Intermediate B   Move body segments in succession from bottom up and top down. This involves bending at the knees, then pushing the hips forward, then arching the back, and then tilting the head back, all in succession. Arms can be incorporated into the skill as well. Body segments should move rhythmically, with a smooth transition from contraction to extension. Show balance and control throughout.

Statics

Statics include those skills where a gymnast's center of gravity is above the base of support and the gymnast is balanced and stable. These types of movements and skills can help athletes develop an understanding of various body positions as well as improve strength, flexibility, and balance. Statics are common elements on the balance beam.

➤ LUNGE

Basic   Place one foot in front of the other foot, and flex at the knee of the front leg, extending the rear leg, with the body upright and weight over both legs. Arms can be held low against the sides of the body, out at side middle, or up by the ears.

➤ RELEVÉ BALANCE

Basic Stand in relevé (on the balls of the feet), with the right foot close behind the left foot. Arms are up by the ears. Hold for two seconds.

➤ FRONT LEANING SUPPORT

Basic From a stand, squat down to place the hands in front of the feet on the beam. Extend the legs backward along the beam toward front support, keeping the arms extended. Keep weight over the feet and arms.

➤ TUCK SIT AND V-SIT

Basic Begin in a straddle-sit position on the beam. Place the hands on the beam behind the hips. For a tuck sit, bend the knees and touch the toes to the beam in front of the hips. For a V-sit, extend the legs in the air in front of the body in a V position.

a

b

c

➤ KNEELING POSE

Intermediate A From a kneeling position, flex one knee and place it on the beam. Turn the back leg so the foot is sideward on the beam. Keep the hands on the beam to balance, and then lift the hands from the beam to an upright balance position.

a

b

c

➤ KNEE SCALE

Intermediate A From a kneeling pose, place the hands on top of the beam in front of the knee, and raise and extend the back leg up from the beam, with arms extended.

➤ ARABESQUE

Intermediate A Stand on one foot with the trunk erect, the support leg in demi-plié. Lift the other foot backward and upward, extending the leg off the beam with the knee facing sideward or down, leg straight. Arms are extended sideward. Maintain balance and control throughout.

➤ PIQUÉ BALANCE

Intermediate A Stand on the beam. Lift one foot up to touch the ankle of the support leg by flexing at the knee of the working leg. Hold this position.

➤ PASSÉ BALANCE

Intermediate B Stand on the beam. Raise one foot up to touch the knee of the support leg by flexing at the knee of the working leg. Hold this position.

➤ SCALE

Intermediate B From a standing position, lift one leg upward and to the rear, lowering the trunk as the rear leg lifts in the air. Keep the leg extended behind the body. The support knee can be flexed.

➤ Y-SCALE

Intermediate B From a standing position, slowly and with control lift one leg to the side. Extend and hold the leg with the hand, either above or below the knee.

➤ SINGLE-LEG LOW SWING-UP

Advanced Squat down and place the hands on the beam in front of the feet. Rise to a pike position. Lift one leg up and back (low), and bring it back down to the beam. The support leg will come slightly off the beam on the other leg's swing up. *Coach's note:* Stack mats up near the level of the top of the beam.

➤ THREE-QUARTER HANDSTAND, SWITCH LEGS

Advanced   From a standing position, lean forward and place the hands on the beam. As one leg swings up in the air, the other leg will come off the beam. Switch legs and land on the opposite foot.

Springs

Athletes must also learn the proper springs, or takeoffs, for the balance beam, which will vary slightly from the positions and technique used for the floor. The width of the balance beam may force the gymnasts to adjust their foot placement. Springs are typically intermediate-level exercises.

➤ BUNNY HOP

Intermediate A   Do small hops on two feet, traveling forward across the balance beam. Show an immediate rebound to the next hop. Maintain a tight body throughout, raise the arms by the ears, keep the legs together, and keep the head up with eyes focused on the end of the beam. This can be done forward, backward, and sideward.

➤ STEP HOP

Intermediate A Step forward on one foot, and hop on that foot, bringing the other foot up in the air. Then step forward and hop on the opposite foot, lifting the free foot into the air. Arms are out to the sides or in opposition during the hop.

➤ LOW STRETCH JUMP

Intermediate B Stand with one foot in front of the other foot. Push off both feet to perform a low stretch jump to land on both feet on the beam in demi-plié. Arms start low at the sides, swing forward and up for the jump, and return to the sides for the finish.

➤ LOW STRIDE LEAP

Intermediate B Push off the beam from one foot to initiate the leap. Land forward on the beam on the other foot in demi-plié. Arms are in opposition or out to the sides during the leap.

➤ LOW TUCK JUMP

Intermediate B Push off from both feet to perform a low tuck jump on the beam, landing on both feet on the beam in demi-plié. Do not grasp the legs. Arms swing forward and up for the jump and come to the sides for the finish.

Rotations

All three types of rotations—vertical, horizontal, and anterior–posterior—are possible on balance beam. Vertical rotations, such as turns, are important first skills for gymnasts to learn. Gymnasts must be able to turn around once they reach the end of the beam. Horizontal rotations, including rolls and saltos, and anterior–posterior rotations, including cartwheels, are usually learned at more intermediate and advanced levels.

ROTATIONS

Vertical Rotations

Movements around the vertical axis running from head to toe are defined as vertical rotations.

➤ LUNGE, 90-DEGREE TURN TO STRADDLE STAND

Basic Stand in lunge position facing the end of the beam. Turn 90 degrees to the side to end in a straddle-stand position facing out. Straighten the right leg at the conclusion of the turn. Arms are at side middle or up by the ears.

➤ PIVOT TURN

Basic   Stand facing the end of the beam, one foot in front of the other. Rise up on the balls of the feet, and turn 180 degrees toward the back foot to face the other end of the beam. Arms are overhead in the crown position.

➤ SQUAT TURN

Intermediate A   Stand facing the end of the beam. Lower to squat position, and turn 180 degrees toward the back foot to face the other end of the beam, in squat position. Arms are overhead in the crown position.

➤ SWING TURN (FOUETTÉ)

Intermediate A Lift one leg up in front, and perform a 180-degree turn on the other foot to finish with the leg up in back of the body in a controlled arabesque position. Lower the leg to the beam to finish in lunge position. Arms swing upward and out to the sides with the turn. Hips and shoulders should remain in alignment throughout. This turn can also be done as a backward swing turn by swinging the leg backward, performing the turn, and finishing with the leg extended in front of the body.

Horizontal Rotations

Movements around the horizontal axis running from one side of the waist to the other are defined as horizontal rotations.

Forward Rolling

Horizontal rotations in a forward direction generate forward rolls.

➤ STRADDLE FORWARD ROLL

Intermediate B   From a straddle-stand position over the low beam (feet are on the floor), place the hands on the beam, tuck the head (chin to chest) and round the back, and place the back of the head and shoulders on the beam between the hands and feet. Hands should support weight as the roll begins. In a slow and controlled manner, roll forward, straight down the beam, coming back up to a straddle-stand position.

➤ FORWARD ROLL

Advanced   From a squat stand, reach forward to place the hands on the beam. Tuck the head and round the back, and place the back of the head and shoulders on the beam between the hands and feet. Push off the feet to initiate the roll. Grasp the beam with the hands during the roll. Step out of the roll through squat stand to straight stand, keeping the arms extended forward and up. *Coach's note:* Spotting is recommended.

Backward Rolling

Horizontal rotations in a backward direction generate backward rolls.

➤ CANDLESTICK

Intermediate B   From a supine (lying) position on the beam, grasp the beam with the hands behind the head, and lift the legs to point the toes toward the ceiling, with weight high on the shoulders. Balance high on the shoulders, with the legs and hips extended so the toes are pointing toward the ceiling.

➤ ROLL BACK AND RETURN TO SIT

Intermediate B   From a tuck sitting position on the beam, roll back to touch the feet over the head on the beam, and then return to a tuck sitting position.

➤ BACK ROLL

Advanced   Start from a tuck or pike sitting position on the beam. Roll back and simultaneously flex at the hips to bring the feet up and over the head. Push with the hands and toes (behind the head) on the beam, and roll over to finish on the hands and shins. Work to finish in tuck position on the balls of the feet. *Coach's note:* Spotting is recommended.

Mounts

A mount is a skill moving from the floor onto an apparatus. Gymnasts must learn how to mount, or climb onto, the balance beam in order to begin training. The skills below are for both basic and intermediate levels.

MOUNTS

➤ STEP ON TO BALANCE STAND

Basic   Stand facing the beam. When first practicing the skill, hands can be placed on the beam; later, the skill can be done hands free. Step up onto the top of the beam with one foot, bringing the other foot up to a balance stand on both feet. Arms can be at side middle or overhead in the crown position.

➤ STEP ON TO SQUAT

Basic   Approach the beam from an oblique angle (side front). The gymnast can use the hand closest to the beam to push off. Step onto the beam with one foot, bring the other foot up to the beam, and lower the body to a squat position with balance and control, facing the end of the beam. Keep the head and torso up, with eyes focused on the end of the beam. Arms can be at side middle or overhead in the crown position.

➤ WOLF MOUNT

Basic   Stand facing the side of the beam. Place the hands on top of the beam and jump off the mat to place one foot between the hands. Then bring the other leg up to place it on top of the beam, outside of the hands, extended toward the end of the beam.

➤ FRONT SUPPORT MOUNT

Intermediate A   Stand facing the side of the beam. Place the hands on top of the beam, and push off the mat to place the front of the thighs against the beam, supporting the body weight with extended arms.

➤ FRONT SUPPORT TO STRADDLE SIT

Intermediate A   From front leaning support position with arms straight and hands shoulder-width apart, swing one leg up and over the side of the beam, turning the body 90 degrees to straddle-sit position on top of the beam, facing the end of the beam. Hands are on the beam in front of the body. The lifted leg should swing fluidly over the beam without resting on it. (If necessary, keep one foot on the mat for balance.)

➤ JUMP TO ONE-FOOT SQUAT SUPPORT

Intermediate A Stand facing the side of the beam. Place the hands on top of the beam, and jump off the mat to place one foot on top of the beam between the hands, leaving the other leg extended beside the beam.

Dismounts

A dismount (or landing) is a skill performed from the apparatus to a controlled landing on the floor. The basic dismounts are vital skills, not only for gymnastics routines but also to help gymnasts understand how to fall and come to the floor safely. These skills are for basic and intermediate levels.

➤ STEP OFF END

Basic From a standing position on the beam, step off the beam to a two-foot landing on the mat in a controlled landing position with arms in front middle.

➤ STRETCH JUMP DISMOUNT

Intermediate A   From a standing position on the beam, jump upward and forward into a stretched position off the end or side of the beam to a two-foot landing on the mat in a controlled landing position with arms in front middle. Use arm swing to assist with the jump, and keep the torso upright and the eyes focused toward the end of the mat.

➤ TUCK JUMP DISMOUNT

Intermediate A   From a standing position on the beam, jump to a tuck position in the air from the end or side of the beam, and land on the mat on two feet in a controlled landing position with arms in middle front.

COACHING TIP   To make dismount jumps more difficult, try different types of jumps, such as straddle jumps; or add twists in the air; or have the gymnast land in a controlled position on the mat and then immediately rebound to a jump turn.

➤ CARTWHEEL TO THREE-QUARTER HANDSTAND DISMOUNT

Intermediate B   From a standing position on the beam, step forward through a lunge position, and lever forward to place the hands sideways on the beam (as for a cartwheel). Push off the base leg to get to a three-quarter handstand. Lower the body to the mat, facing the beam. Maintain a grasp on the beam through landing. *Coach's note:* Spotting is recommended.

Gymnastics meets provide the opportunity for your athletes to

show what they've learned in practice. Just as your athletes' focus shifts on meet days from learning and practicing to competing, your focus shifts from teaching skills to coaching athletes as they perform those skills in competition. Of course, a gymnastics meet is a teaching opportunity as well, but the focus is on performing what has been learned, participating, and having fun.

In previous chapters, you learned how to teach your gymnasts skills; in this chapter, you will learn how to coach your gymnasts as they execute those skills in gymnastics meets. We provide coaching principles that will guide you before, during, and after the competition.

Before the Meet

Many coaches focus on how they will coach only during the actual meet, when instead preparations should begin well before the gymnast salutes the judges. Ideally, a day or two before a meet, you should cover several things—in addition to techniques and tactics—to prepare your athletes. Depending on the age group you are working with, you will need to create a specific plan for the upcoming meet based on information that is available to you. This will include registering for the meet and making decisions on specific tactics that you want your team to use. You should also discuss particulars such as what to eat before the meet, what to wear, what to bring, and when to be at the gym.

Entering Your Athletes for the Meet

Meet directors have different systems for managing entries. Systems vary depending on the meet, but most share many similarities. Let's look at some of the common factors of meet entries.

For all USA Gymnastics–sanctioned competitions, entries are required in advance. Sometimes the coach must fill out a form listing the name, date of birth, competitive level, and USA Gymnastics member number for each gymnast, which is faxed or mailed to the meet director. Increasingly, meet directors are using online systems to handle entries. These systems require the coach to go online to a designated Web site and complete the entry process. Following are some general considerations regarding meet entries:

- Read all premeet information from the host club or meet director carefully.
- There is always an entry deadline. Failure to meet the deadline could result in fines or may preclude the gymnasts' participation.
- Ensure all birthdates and levels are listed correctly on the registration form because this is how the gymnasts will be grouped into sessions at the meet.

- Look over the meet information and schedule of events, and think carefully about entries as well as your team's tactical preparations. Factors such as equipment, age groups, and team competition may cause you to adjust your entries or choose a different meet.
- If a team competition is available, include your team's entry.
- Pay all entry fees when you register or by the deadline.

COACHING TIP Before athletes can be entered in a meet, they must have an active athlete membership with USA Gymnastics. The athlete membership application process opens in June for the season running August 1 through July 31 each year. The coach or club administrators are responsible for gathering completed athlete membership application forms from the athletes and their parents and registering the athletes with USA Gymnastics. This should be done early in the season (as close to August 1 as possible) so that the athletes receive a full year's worth of benefits for their membership. This also avoids any last-minute rush fees to process an athlete membership before a competition. Remember that coaches must also be USA Gymnastics members in order to coach on the floor of a sanctioned competition. Be sure your membership and all requirements are up to date.

Deciding Team Tactics

Tactics are strategies you may employ while training before a meet or during the actual competition. When developing your plan, keep in mind that your gymnasts need to understand what you expect of them during the meet. Take time at the beginning or end of each practice to discuss these expectations. This is especially important for gymnasts who are competing for the first time. During the week before a meet, you should talk about tactics and other issues related to the competition. Depending on the age level, experience, and knowledge of your athletes, you may want to let them help you determine tactics and competition strategies. It is the coach's role to help youngsters grow through the sport experience. Allowing athlete input helps the children learn the sport and involves them at a planning level often reserved solely for the coach. It also gives them a feeling of ownership. Rather than just "carrying out orders" for the coach, they're executing the plan that they helped develop. Youngsters who have a say in how they approach a task often respond with more enthusiasm and motivation.

Following a training plan leading up to competition, practicing on competition-like surfaces, making the training environment more like the competition environment, deciding on the landing surfaces to be used at the meet, and arranging your team lineup (if needed) are all tactics that should be considered and communicated to your gymnasts.

Discussing Premeet Details

Athletes need to know what to do before a meet, such as what they should eat on meet day and when, what clothing they should wear to the meet, what equipment they should bring, what time they should arrive, and what kind of warm-up they should do. You should discuss these particulars with them at the last practice before a meet. Here are some guidelines for discussing these issues.

COACHING TIP You should have a preset plan or routine that is used before every meet. This can help alleviate nerves and build confidence, especially for gymnasts in younger age groups. A premeet routine will also help athletes forget outside concerns and get into the frame of mind to focus on competition.

Premeet Meal

In general, the goal for the premeet meal is to fuel the athlete for the upcoming competition, to maximize carbohydrate stores, and to provide energy for the brain. Some foods digest more quickly than others, such as carbohydrate and protein, so we suggest that athletes consume these rather than fat, which digests more slowly. Good carbohydrate foods include spaghetti, rice, and bran. Good protein foods include low-fat yogurt and skinless chicken. Athletes should eat foods they are familiar with and that they know they can digest easily. Big meals should be eaten three to four hours before the meet. Athletes who don't have time for a big meal may use sports beverages and meal-replacement bars, but these shouldn't be used regularly as a replacement for the premeet meal.

The meet time will also affect the type of meal your gymnasts should consume. If the gymnastics meet starts right after school or early in the morning on the weekend, it won't be possible or practical for your gymnasts to eat three to four hours before the meet. In these situations, a lighter snack or breakfast will be more appropriate.

COACHING TIP Gymnastics meets are often all-day events. Therefore, you need to help your gymnasts stay hydrated and fueled throughout the competition, not just before. For longer competitions, consider working with parents to rotate the responsibility for providing water or sports drinks, along with nutritious snacks such as fruit or crackers. See chapter 4 for guidelines on how much fluid your gymnasts should drink before, during, and after a meet.

Clothing and Equipment

Unless the team is traveling a long distance to compete, you should typically require that your athletes arrive in their team uniform: a warm-up leotard (girls) or shorts and T-shirt (boys) and warm-up suit. The gymnasts can change into their competitive leotards at the end of the warm-up period. Athletes will need to bring their own hand grips, floor exercise music, and any other personal equipment needed. An athletic tape supply is also helpful because it may not be readily available from the meet director. Be sure to discuss equipment expectations at the preseason parent orientation meeting (as described in chapter 2).

COACHING TIP Working together with your gymnasts to pick the style of your team warm-ups or leotards can provide an excellent team bonding activity.

Make sure that eyeglasses fit snugly on any athletes wearing them. If they don't, ask parents to provide their children with an elastic sport strap to hold the glasses in place. Athletes are allowed to wear braces or protective wraps to prevent injury or to protect current injuries, as long as the athletes are cleared by a doctor to participate. You should ask parents to ensure that their children bring the required items when they come to the meet.

Arrival Time

You should instruct your athletes to arrive 15 to 30 minutes before the scheduled general warm-up time. This will allow the gymnasts to arrive at the facility, orient themselves, get checked in, and change if necessary before the start of the warm-up period.

COACHING TIP Although the meet director has the formal responsibilities for facilities, you should know what to look for to ensure that the environment is safe for all athletes (see the "Sample Facility Inspection Form" in the appendix on page 241). Arrive at the gym before your athletes, check in with the meet director and officials, check the apparatus and equipment, and greet your athletes as they arrive.

Warm-Up

Athletes need to both physically and mentally prepare for a competition. Physical preparation involves warming up. We suggest that athletes utilize the general warm-up and event warm-up periods provided.

Warm-ups on meet day should be similar to warm-ups done at practice. You should let the athletes know where they are allowed to warm up in the gym. Some facilities require warm-ups to be done in adjacent areas. The warm-up should consist of brief aerobic activity (e.g., running), stretches that focus on range of motion, and a few brief drills related to skill rehearsals.

You should refrain from delivering a long-winded pep talk, but you can help athletes mentally prepare for the competition by reminding them of the skills they've been working on in recent practices and by focusing their attention on their strengths and what they've been doing well. Also take time to remind athletes that they should support their teammates, compete hard and smart, and have fun!

COACHING TIP   A gymnastics club may establish a base camp, especially at large invitational meets. The coaches, parents, and gymnasts congregate in one central area. The team uses this base camp as a meeting place and a spot to store bags and gear. The parents and noncompeting gymnasts remain in the base camp area while the coaches and competing gymnasts are on the field of play. Additionally, the group can help cheer on all members of the team.

Unplanned Events

Part of being prepared to coach is to expect the unexpected. What do you do if athletes are late? What if *you* have an emergency and can't make the meet or will be late? What if the meet setup or equipment is different from what you expected? Being prepared to handle out-of-the-ordinary circumstances will help you when unplanned events happen.

Communicating With Parents

The groundwork for your communication with parents will have been laid in the parent orientation meeting, where the parents learned the best ways to support their kids'—and the whole team's—efforts in the gym. You should encourage parents to judge success based not just on the outcome of the events but also on how the kids are improving their performances.

If parents criticize the kids for mistakes made during the meet, make disparaging remarks about the officials or opponents, or shout instructions on which techniques to focus on, you should ask them to refrain and to instead show support for the team through their comments and actions. These standards of conduct should all be covered in the preseason parent orientation meeting.

When time permits, as parents gather before a meet (and before the team has begun formal preparations for the competition), you can let them know in a general sense what the team has been focusing on during the past week and what your goals are for the meet. However, your gymnasts must come first during this time, so focus on your gymnasts during the premeet warm-up.

After a meet, quickly come together as a coaching staff and decide what to say to the team. Then, if the opportunity arises, you can informally assess with parents how the gymnasts did based not on the outcome but on meeting performance goals and competing to the best of their abilities. Help parents see the contest as a process, not solely as a test that is pass or fail, win or lose. Encourage parents to reinforce that concept at home. For more information on communicating with parents, see page 16 in chapter 2.

If athletes are late, you may need to adjust their warm-up or scratch them from the meet. Therefore, you should stress to your gymnasts that there are important reasons for being on time. First, part of being a member of a team is being committed to and responsible for the other members. When athletes don't show up, or show up late, they break that commitment. And second, athletes need to go through a warm-up to physically prepare for the competition. Skipping the warm-up increases the risk of injury.

There may be a time when an emergency causes you to be late or to miss a meet. In these cases, you should notify another member of your coaching staff, if you have one, and the meet director. If notified in advance, a volunteer or a parent of an athlete might be able to help with registration and premeet organization until you arrive.

Sometimes apparatus or equipment, the meet setup, or the schedule may be different from what was communicated in the premeet information. If you learn of these changes before meet day, it is helpful to let your athletes and their parents know in advance. If you are notified during registration at the event, gather your athletes and explain the changes and any adjustments they will need to make.

During the Meet

Throughout the meet, you must keep the competition in proper perspective and help your gymnasts do the same. Observe how your athletes execute the routines, meet plans, and tactics. These observations will help you decide on appropriate practice plans for the following week and give you important information for feedback to the athletes. Let's take a more detailed look at your responsibilities during a meet.

Keeping a Proper Perspective

Winning is the short-term goal of your gymnastics program. The long-term goals are helping your athletes learn gymnastics skills and rules of the sport, how to become fit, and how to exhibit good sportsmanship in the gym and in life. Your young athletes are winning when they are becoming better human beings through their participation in gymnastics. Maintain this outlook when you coach. You have the privilege of setting the tone for how your team approaches the gymnastics meet. Keep winning and all aspects of the competition in proper perspective, and your young charges will likely follow suit.

Tactical Decisions

You will need to make tactical decisions in several areas throughout a meet. You'll make decisions about apparatus settings and landing mats, about making slight adjustments to your gymnasts' technique, and about dealing with gymnasts' performance errors. In some instances, coaches may also need to make decisions about what skills a gymnast will complete.

Apparatus Settings and Landing Mat Selections

If you arrive at the meet site and notice that the brand of apparatus and equipment is different from that in your gym or that certain types of optional landing mats are not available, do not panic. Talk to your gymnasts about the differences and similarities of the apparatus and equipment. Make sure the gymnasts feel comfortable on the apparatus during the warm-up period, and be encouraging. Remind them of the stability and safety of the equipment and to focus on their skills rather than the feel of different equipment. As needed, work with the gymnasts to make technical adjustments to better compensate for equipment performance and variance.

Correcting Errors

In chapter 6, you learned about two types of errors: learning errors and performance errors. Learning errors occur because athletes don't know how to perform a skill. Performance errors are made not because athletes don't know how to execute the skill but because they make mistakes in carrying out what they do know.

Sometimes it's not easy to tell which type of error athletes are making. Knowing your athletes' capabilities helps you determine if they know the skill and are simply making mistakes in executing it or if they don't know how to perform it. If they are making learning errors—that is, they don't know how to perform the skills—you should note this and cover it at the next practice. Competition is usually not the best time to teach skills.

If your gymnasts are making performance errors, however, you can help them correct those errors during a meet. Athletes who make performance errors often do so because they have a lapse in concentration or motivation, or they are simply demonstrating human error. Competition can also adversely affect a young athlete's technique, and a word of encouragement about concentration may help. If you do correct a performance error during a meet, do so in a quiet, controlled, and positive tone of voice between routines.

For those making performance errors, you must determine if the error is just an occasional error that anyone can make or if it is an expected error for a youngster at that stage of development. If the latter is the case, then the gymnast may appreciate your not commenting on the mistake. The gymnast knows it was a mistake and may already know how to correct it. On the other hand, perhaps an encouraging word and a coaching cue (e.g., "Stretch into the back walkover") may be just what the gymnast needs. Knowing your athletes and what to say is very much a part of the art of coaching.

Adjusting Skills

In some cases, an athlete may be unprepared to complete a certain skill in the given competition or, because of anxiety or other factors, may suddenly have serious trouble with a skill that is usually performed well. Watch your gymnasts closely during the warm-up period. If you notice an athlete having such problems, consider changing or removing that skill from the athlete's routine for this competition. Remember, your gymnasts' safety should be the number one priority.

Coach and Athlete Behavior

Another aspect of coaching on meet day is managing behavior—both yours and your athletes'. As a coach, it is your responsibility to control emotions when the gymnastics meet is not going the way that you or your athletes would have hoped.

Coach Conduct

You very much influence your gymnasts' behavior before, during, and after a meet. If you're up, your gymnasts are more likely to be up. If you're anxious, they'll take notice, and the anxiety can become contagious. If you're negative, they'll respond with worry. If you're positive, they'll compete with more enjoyment. If you're constantly yelling instructions or commenting on mistakes and errors, it will be difficult for athletes to concentrate. Instead, you should let athletes get into the flow of the competition.

The focus should be on positive competition and on having fun. A coach who overorganizes everything and dominates a meet from the side of the gym is definitely not making the event fun. So how should you conduct yourself? Here are a few pointers:

- Be calm, in control, and supportive of your gymnasts.

- Encourage athletes often, but instruct during competition sparingly. Athletes should focus on their performance during competition, not on instructions shouted from the sidelines.

- If you need to instruct a gymnast, do so in an unobtrusive manner when you're standing near each other. Never yell at athletes for making a mistake. Instead, briefly demonstrate or remind them of the correct technique, and encourage them. Tell them how to correct the problem when it is their turn to compete again.

You should also discuss meet demeanor as a coaching staff, making sure everyone is in agreement regarding proper conduct in the gym. Once these expectations are agreed on, stick with them. Remember, you're not competing for an Olympic gold medal! At this level, gymnastics meets are designed to help children develop their skills and themselves—and to have fun. So coach in a manner at meets that helps your gymnasts achieve these objectives.

Athlete Conduct

You're responsible for keeping your athletes under control. Do so by setting a good example and by disciplining when necessary. Set team rules for good behavior. If athletes attempt to cheat, argue, badger others, yell disparaging remarks, and the like, it is your responsibility to correct the misbehavior. Initially, this may mean removing gymnasts immediately from the competition, letting them calm down, and then speaking to them quietly, explaining that their behavior is not acceptable for your team—and that if they want to compete, they must not repeat the action. You must remember, too, that younger athletes are still learning how to deal with their emotions in addition to learning the sport. As a coach, you must strive to remain calm during times when young athletes are having trouble controlling their emotions.

Consider having team rules in these areas of conduct:

- Athlete language
- Athlete behavior
- Interactions with officials
- Discipline for misbehavior
- Dress code for competitions

Athlete Welfare

All athletes are not the same. Some attach their self-worth to winning and losing. This idea is fueled by coaches, parents, peers, and others in society who place great emphasis on winning. Athletes become anxious when they're uncertain whether they can meet the expectations of others—especially when meeting a particular expectation is important to them also.

If your gymnasts look uptight during a meet, find ways to reduce both the uncertainties about how their performance will be evaluated and the importance they are attaching to competition. Help gymnasts focus on realistic personal goals—goals that are reachable and measurable and that will help them improve their performance while having fun as they compete. Another way to reduce anxiety on meet day is to avoid emotional premeet pep talks. Instead, remind gymnasts of the techniques and strategies they will use, and urge them to compete hard, to do their best, and to have fun.

When coaching during meets, remember that the most important outcome of participating in gymnastics is building or enhancing athletes' self-worth. Keep that firmly in mind, and strive to promote this through every coaching decision.

Opponents and Officials

You must respect opponents and officials. Without them, there wouldn't be a competition. Opponents provide opportunities for your team to test itself, improve, and excel. Officials help provide a fair and safe experience for athletes and, as appropriate, help them learn the sport.

Keeping the Meet Safe

Chapter 4 is devoted to safety, but it's worth noting here that safety during meets can be affected by how the meet director and the officials run the meet. If things are not organized well and this puts your gymnasts at risk of injury, you must intervene. Voice your concerns in a respectful manner, and place the emphasis where it should be—on the athletes' safety. One of an official's main responsibilities is to ensure safety. Both you and the officials are working together to protect the athletes whenever possible. Don't hesitate to address an issue of safety with an official when the need arises.

MEET DAY

You and your athletes should show respect for opponents and officials by giving your best efforts and being civil. Don't allow your athletes to "trash talk" or taunt a competitor or an official. Such behavior is disrespectful to the spirit of competition, and you should immediately remove an athlete from a meet (as discussed previously in "Athlete Conduct") if that athlete disobeys your team rules in this area.

Remember, too, that officials receive training and must meet certain criteria, but they are not always perfect. Although they are working in the best interest of the sport and its participants, mistakes may sometimes happen. Officials do their best to score and rank the gymnasts properly.

After the Meet

When the meet is over, join your gymnasts in congratulating the coaches and gymnasts of the opposing teams, and then be sure to thank the officials. Check on any injuries, and inform the gymnasts about how to care for them. Be prepared to speak with the officials about any problems that occurred during the meet. Then, hold a brief team meeting to ensure that your gymnasts are on an even keel, whether they met their goals or not.

Reactions After a Meet

Your first concern after a meet should be your athletes' attitudes and mental well-being. You don't want them to be too high after a first-place finish or too low after a poor performance. This is the time you can be most influential in helping athletes keep the outcome in perspective and settle their emotions.

When your gymnasts are celebrating great performances, make sure they do so in a way that doesn't show disrespect for the other competitors. It's okay and appropriate to be happy and celebrate a great result, but don't allow your gymnasts to taunt the opponents or boast about their victory. If an athlete loses a close competition, the athlete will naturally be disappointed. But if your gymnast has made a winning effort, let the gymnast know this. After a loss, help gymnasts keep their chins up and maintain a positive attitude that will carry over into the next practice and contest. Winning and losing are a part of life, not just a part of sport. If athletes can handle both equally well, they'll be successful in whatever they do.

Postmeet Team Meeting

After the meet, gather your team in a designated area for a short meeting. Before this meeting, decide as a coaching staff what to say and who will say it. Be sure the staff speaks with one voice after the meet.

COACHING TIP Before conducting the postmeet team meeting, you should lead your gymnasts through a cool-down similar to the one you use to end your practice sessions. This will not only help gymnasts improve their flexibility but also help them calm down after the meet so they can focus on what you are about to say. The younger the athletes, the shorter your postmeet cool-down and team meeting should be. For athletes wh85o are 10 and under, keep the postmeet routine to no more than 10 minutes; for older athletes, keep it to no more than 15 minutes.

If your athletes have performed well in a meet, you should compliment them and congratulate them. Tell them specifically what they did well, whether they won or lost. This will reinforce their desire to repeat their good performances. Don't use this time to criticize individual athletes for poor performances in front of teammates, and don't go over technical problems and adjustments, either. You should help athletes improve their skills, but do so at the next practice. Immediately after a meet, athletes won't absorb much technical information.

Finally, make sure your gymnasts have transportation home. Be the last one to leave in order to ensure full supervision of your gymnasts.

Developing Season and Practice Plans

We hope you've learned a lot from this book: what your responsibilities are as a coach, how to communicate well and provide for safety, how to teach and shape skills, and how to coach during competitions. But competitions make up only a portion of your season—you and your gymnasts will spend more time in practices than in competition. How well you conduct practices and prepare your gymnasts for competition will greatly affect not only their enjoyment and success throughout the season but also your own.

Season Plans

Your season plan acts as a snapshot of the entire season. Before the first practice with your athletes, you must sit down as a coaching staff and develop such a plan. To do so, simply write down each practice and meet date on a calendar, and then go back and number the practices. These practice numbers are the foundation of your season plan. First, imagine the kind of fitness you would like your gymnasts to demonstrate at the end of the season. Also imagine the kind of training the team will do during the final weeks leading up to the most important championship. Then, moving backward from practice to practice, outline a systematic progression that will lead to those fitness and training goals. Determine what you will cover in each practice and what kind of training will be done. Note the purpose of the practice, the main skills you will cover, and the activities you will use.

Fun Learning Environment

Regardless of what point you're at in your season, you should work to create an environment that welcomes learning and promotes long-term development. Following are seven tips to help you and your coaching staff get the most out of your practices:

1. Stick to the practice times agreed on as a staff.
2. Start each practice with an appropriate warm-up.
3. Keep the practice routine as consistent as possible so that the athletes can feel comfortable.
4. Be organized in your approach by moving quickly from one activity to another and from one stage of training to another.
5. Tell your athletes what the practice will include before the practice starts.
6. Allow the athletes to take water breaks whenever possible.
7. Focus on providing positive feedback.

In gymnastics, coaches generally use an approach to training called *periodization*. Periodization simply means that the year or season is divided into periods, each with a specific training goal. In the classic model, the year or season is broken into three periods: rest or off-season, preparation period, and competition period. The preparation and competition periods are then broken down further into two phases. The preparation period is divided into general and specific preparation, and the competition period is divided into early competitions and championships.

Ideally, the preparation period will be about half of the overall training for the year. This is not always practical depending on the length of the competition season; however, the spirit of the early practices should be very general, and the goal is to prepare the whole body for the more specific training to come. The idea is to get a higher volume of work in to build overall fitness. This means that the intensity must remain moderate or low. Here are some examples of general preparation activities:

- Body-position shapes and holds (e.g., hollow hold, arch hold, tuck, pike, and layout)
- Core stability work
- General strength conditioning (e.g., sit-ups, push-ups, pull-ups, and bar hangs)
- Flexibility development (both static and dynamic)
- Landing and falling drills and techniques
- Basic skills on each event (e.g., running and hurdling on vault; swings and pullovers on bars; balance beam complexes; and rolls, cartwheels, and handstands on floor)

As athletes begin to get into shape, preparation can become more specific to the events of gymnastics. This is when the coach begins to help athletes figure out the techniques and develop the movement patterns that are related to successful completion of gymnastics skills and routines. Although the training begins to look more like what will happen in competition, the primary goal is still to improve fitness, with a secondary aim of learning skills. The overall volume remains high, and the intensity remains moderate. Here are some examples of specific preparation:

- Learning and practicing the designated skills on each event, based on the level
- Practicing multiple skills together in a series
- Doing half routines
- Performing dance-through routines (omitting tumbling passes) on floor
- Practicing dismounts and landings on softer landing surfaces
- Continuing landing drills
- Conditioning for strength, cardiorespiratory endurance, and flexibility

In early meets, gymnasts begin to put together the skills they will use in competition. It is okay for gymnasts to go to the first few meets with imperfect technique. The championship meets at the end of the season are the ones that matter most. Early gymnastics meets play a major part of the overall training. During this period, intensity of training begins to increase, and consequently, volume must be decreased. Work is more focused on mastering technique. Here are some of the things that happen during the early part of the competitive period:

- Full routines performed in practice
- Multiple routines performed back to back
- More emphasis on correctly performing skills
- Mock competitions
- Competitions

Finally, as the season nears completion, the championship meets arrive. In some cases, gymnasts might have three or four championship-type meets. In other cases, there will be only one championship meet at the end of the season. During this period, it is too late to develop new levels of fitness, and the focus of training is perfecting technique and executing high-level efforts. Rest is critical at this point. Because the gymnasts are used to more training volume, they may get a bit restless now that they have less work to do. As the coach, you must encourage the gymnasts to use their extra energy when it counts—at the championship meet. Activities during the championship phase include the following:

- Video analysis
- Planning sessions to address tactics and strategy
- High-intensity, low-volume training sessions with large rest intervals
- Drills and simulations of competition environment
- Traveling to high-level competitions and competing for lifetime-best results

COACHING TIP While developing your season plan, keep in mind that you will want to incorporate the guided discovery approach into your practices (see chapter 5). The guided discovery approach focuses on replicating the competitive environment. When appropriate, using modified competitive activities better prepares the gymnasts, both physically and mentally, for the demands of competition. This can be as simple as tailoring the repetitions based on quality, such as asking for three hit beam routines. A more elaborate setup would be to stage a mock competition with judges. This is a lower-pressure situation that still simulates the competition atmosphere for the gymnasts. They can practice their routines as well as other competition etiquette.

Following is more detailed information about season plans for each particular level—levels 1 to 3, level 4, and levels 5 and 6.

Season Plan Considerations for Levels 1 to 3

Most children at levels 1 to 3 have had little or no exposure to gymnastics. Don't assume that they have a great deal of knowledge of the sport. Help them explore the basic skills, such as jumping and landing, rolls, turns, handstands, cartwheels, and swinging. Keep practices playful throughout the entire season. Use many different training activities during each session. Try to design the activities so that children stay active and have plenty of opportunities to participate. Standing in line while waiting for a turn makes it difficult for children to stay engaged. Technique should be introduced in a fundamentally sound fashion. However, the natural style that children bring to gymnastics is often perfectly acceptable. Although children at these levels have the opportunity to participate in shows and competitions, the main focus should be on participation, learning the rules, and having fun. See the sample season plan for beginners (level 1) on page 220.

Season Plan Considerations for Level 4

Children at level 4 can begin training with a bit more specificity. However, the coach should try to make sure that the practices are fun and that children are engaged. It is too early to make practices into serious workouts. Children can be challenged and begin some organized training, but a general and fun approach should be used. Development of postural strength must take place before a detailed approach to technique can be emphasized. See the sample season plan for gymnasts at level 4 starting on page 222.

Season Plan Considerations for Levels 5 and 6

At these levels, gymnasts are building on the skills they have learned in years past and adding more skills on each event. Postural strength should be developed to the point where gymnasts can demonstrate some mastery of technique. Gymnasts can benefit from more intense and structured training. Competitions begin to get more serious, including greater opportunities for advancement. Nevertheless, gymnasts at this age, though they may act grown up, are still very young. If training becomes too rigorous and serious, or competitions become too intense, gymnasts may begin to lose interest in the sport.

SAMPLE SEASON PLAN, LEVEL 1 GIRLS

Session: 1

Welcome • Warm-up • Attendance • Safety review • Practice agenda

Week 1	Week 2	Week 3	Week 4	Week 5	Week 6	Week 7	Week 8
Warm-up 1. Jumping jacks 2. Basic body positions, stretching 3. Rules and safety	**Warm-up** 1. Running 2. Basic body positions, stretching	**Warm-up** 1. Aerobic game 2. Basic body positions, stretching	**Warm-up** 1. Song and dance 2. Basic body positions, stretching	**Warm-up** 1. Jumping jacks 2. Basic body positions, stretching	**Warm-up** 1. Running 2. Basic body positions, stretching	**Warm-up** 1. Aerobic game 2. Basic body positions, stretching	**Warm-up** 1. Song and dance 2. Basic body positions, stretching
Floor 1. Safe landing position 2. Line drills: locomotor skills 3. Basic tumbling: rolls	**Floor** 1. Basic tumbling: cartwheels 2. Stations (statics): holds, headstands, handstands	**Floor** 1. Line drills: springs, landings, turns 2. Basic tumbling: rolls	**Floor** 1. Basic tumbling: cartwheels 2. Stations: bridges, walkovers, limbers on barrel	**Floor** 1. Line drills: locomotor skills 2. Basic tumbling: rolls, cartwheels	**Floor** 1. Basic tumbling: rolls, cartwheels 2. Stations (statics): holds, headstands, handstands	**Floor** 1. Line drills: springs, landings, turns 2. Basic tumbling: rolls, cartwheels	**Floor** 1. Basic tumbling: rolls, cartwheels 2. Stations: bridges, walkovers, limbers
Bars 1. Proper landings 2. Grips 3. Hangs 4. Pullover, forward roll to dismount 5. Strength	**Bars** 1. Walks 2. Pivot turns 3. Jumping off and landing 4. Proper landing, safety roll	**Trampoline** 1. Straight, tuck, straddle jumps 2. Seat drops 3. Doggy drops 4. Conditioning	**Vault** 1. Squat on, jump off 2. Hurdle onto target 3. Straddle onto Resi-Pit, forward roll 4. Strength	**Beam** 1. Varied walks 2. Small jumps 3. Three-quarter handstands 4. Dismounts	**Bars** 1. Hangs 2. Swings 3. Pullover, forward roll to dismount 4. Squat on floor bar	**Trampoline** 1. Jump turns 2. Seat drops 3. Doggy drops 4. Conditioning	**Bars** 1. Stride supports 2. Casts 3. Back hip circles 4. Strength

Vault	Tumbling trampoline	Bars	Beam	Vault	Tumbling trampoline	Beam	Vault
1. Proper landing, safety roll 2. Running drills 3. Hurdle onto board 4. Squat-on drills	1. Jump series 2. Conditioning	1. Swings 2. Holds 3. Cast back to bar and dismount 4. Strength	1. Varied walks 2. Static holds 3. Levers 4. Cartwheels (low)	1. Running drills 2. Hurdle onto board, jump 3. Jump from vault table 4. Pike onto Resi-Pit, forward roll	1. Jump series 2. Dive rolls 3. Conditioning	1. Varied walks 2. Jumps 3. Static holds 4. Cartwheels (low)	1. Rebound, jump, jump, land 2. Squat on, jump off 3. Handstand, fall to back 4. Strength
Cool-down 1. Partner activity 2. Stretching	**Cool-down** 1. Stretching	**Cool-down** 1. Relay game 2. Stretching	**Cool-down** 1. Obstacle course 2. Stretching	**Cool-down** 1. Stretching	**Cool-down** 1. Partner activity 2. Stretching	**Cool-down** 1. Relay game 2. Stretching	**Cool-down** 1. Obstacle course 2. Stretching

Closure • Handouts • Talk with parents

© USA Gymnastics

SAMPLE SEASON PLAN, LEVEL 4 GIRLS

Session: Preseason

	Week 1		Week 2		Week 3	
	Day 1	Day 2	Day 1	Day 2	Day 1	Day 2
	Welcome • Warm-up • Attendance • Safety review • Practice agenda					
	Warm-up 1. Jumping jacks 2. Conditioning 3. Basic stretching 4. Rules and safety review	**Warm-up** 1. Running 2. Conditioning 3. Basic stretching	**Warm-up** 1. Aerobic game 2. Conditioning 3. Basic stretching	**Warm-up** 1. Song and dance 2. Conditioning 3. Basic stretching	**Warm-up** 1. Jumping jacks 2. Conditioning 3. Basic stretching	**Warm-up** 1. Running 2. Conditioning 3. Basic stretching
	Floor 1. Line drills (locomotor): rolls, cartwheels 2. Stations: round-offs, bridges, limbers 3. Leaps and jumps	**Beam** 1. Beam complex 2. Static holds 3. Jumps 4. Handstands 5. V-sit swing to push-up position 6. Cartwheels	**Floor** 1. Tumbling stations: round-offs, back handsprings, walkovers, limbers 2. Leaps and jumps 3. Turns 4. Choreography	**Trampoline** 1. Jumps 2. Drops 3. Turns 4. Back saltos 5. Conditioning	**Vault** 1. Running drills 2. Hurdle and rebound 3. Donkey kicks 4. Handstand on raised surface, fall to back 5. Handstand blocks and holds	**Floor** 1. Choreography and dance 2. Turns 3. Tumbling stations: round-offs, back handsprings, walkovers, limbers
	Bars 1. Pullovers 2. Casts 3. Back hip circles 4. Squat on, jump off 5. Swing half turns 6. Strength	**Tumbling trampoline** 1. Jump series 2. Round-off rebounds 3. Dive rolls 4. Forward saltos 5. Conditioning	**Vault** 1. Running drills 2. Jumps (various shapes) to stuck landing 3. Handstand blocks and holds 4. Handstand on raised surface, fall to back	**Floor** 1. Line drills (locomotor): rolls, cartwheels, bridges, limbers 2. Leaps and jumps 3. Back roll to push-up position 4. Round-offs, handsprings	**Beam** 1. Beam complex 2. Static holds 3. Turns 4. Handstands 5. Mounts 6. Dismounts	**Bars** 1. Glide, pullover 2. Front hip circle to cast 3. Single-leg squat-through, stride circle 4. Cast, underswing dismount 5. Strength

Vault	Bars	Beam	Bars	Tumbling trampoline	Vault
1. Running drills	1. Glide swings	1. Beam complex	1. Squat on and single-leg squat-through	1. Jump series	1. Running drills
2. Hurdle and rebound	2. Inverted holds	2. Mounts: front supports, leg swings	2. Glide swings	2. Back handspring, rebound	2. Jumping
3. Forward roll onto mat stack	3. Kick to handstand	3. V-sit swing to tuck stand	3. Inverted holds	3. Round-offs, back handsprings	3. Handstand blocks and holds
4. Handstand, fall to back	4. Single-leg cut, stride circle, cut back	4. Leaps and jumps	4. Casts	4. Conditioning	4. Forward roll onto mat stack
5. Handstand holds	5. Pullover, front support, fall back to inverted hang	5. Handstand dismount to push-up position	5. Front hip circles		5. Handstand on raised surface, fall to back
	6. Strength		6. Strength		
Cool-down	**Cool-down**	**Cool-down**	**Cool-down**	**Cool-down**	**Cool-down**
1. Partner activity	1. Relay game	1. Fitness game	1. Skill contest	1. Partner activity	1. Fitness game
2. Stretching	2. Stretching	2. Stretching	2. Stretching	2. Stretching	2. Stretching

Closure • Handouts • Talk with parents

> continued

223

SAMPLE SEASON PLAN, LEVEL 4 GIRLS (continued)

Welcome • Warm-up • Attendance • Safety Review • Practice Agenda

	Week 4		Week 5		Week 6	
	Day 1	Day 2	Day 1	Day 2	Day 1	Day 2
	Warm-up 1. Aerobic game 2. Conditioning 3. Basic stretching	**Warm-up** 1. Song and dance 2. Conditioning 3. Basic stretching	**Warm-up** 1. Jumping jacks 2. Conditioning 3. Basic stretching	**Warm-up** 1. Running 2. Conditioning 3. Basic stretching	**Warm-up** 1. Aerobic game 2. Conditioning 3. Basic stretching	**Warm-up** 1. Song and dance 2. Conditioning 3. Basic stretching
	Beam 1. Beam complex 2. Leaps and jumps 3. Cartwheels 4. V-sit swing to squat stand 5. Turns 6. Cartwheels	**Bars** 1. Single-leg squat-through, stride circle 2. Cast, back hip circle 3. Front hip circle, cast 4. Underswing dismounts 5. Inverted holds 6. Strength	**Floor** 1. Tumbling stations 2. Half floor routines: first half, then second half	**Beam** 1. Beam complex 2. Half beam routines: first half, then second half 3. Handstands 4. Dismounts	**Floor** 1. Line drills 2. Leaps and jumps 3. Half floor routines: first half, then second half	**Trampoline** 1. Jumps 2. Drops 3. Turns 4. Back saltos 5. Conditioning
	Trampoline 1. Jumps 2. Drops 3. Turns 4. Back saltos 5. Conditioning	**Vault** 1. Running drills 2. Hurdle and rebound 3. Donkey kicks 4. Handstand block to back 5. Handstand on raised surface, fall to back	**Bars** 1. Routine: first half 2. Casts 3. Back hip circles 4. Underswing dismounts 5. Strength	**Tumbling trampoline** 1. Jump series 2. Back handspring, rebound 3. Round off, back handspring 4. Conditioning	**Vault** 1. Running drills 2. Jumps (various shapes) to stuck landing 3. Handstand blocks and holds 4. Handstand on raised surface, fall to back	**Floor** 1. Tumbling stations 2. Full and half floor routines

Floor	Beam	Vault	Bars	Beam	Bars
1. Line drills (locomotor): rolls, cartwheels, bridges, limbers 2. Leaps and jumps 3. Back roll to push-up position 4. Round offs, back handsprings	1. Beam complex 2. Static holds and steps 3. Mounts 4. Dismounts 5. Handstands 6. Rolls	1. Running drills 2. Hurdle and rebound 3. Forward roll onto mat stack 4. Handstand fall to back 5. Handstand blocks and holds	1. Routine: second half 2. Glides 3. Pullovers 4. Front hip circles 5. Strength	1. Beam complex 2. Half beam routines: first half, then second half 3. Mounts 4. Cartwheels	1. Full and half bar routines 2. Work problem areas 3. Strength
Cool-down 1. Relay game 2. Stretching	**Cool-down** 1. Skill contest 2. Stretching	**Cool-down** 1. Partner activity 2. Stretching	**Cool-down** 1. Fitness game 2. Stretching	**Cool-down** 1. Relay game 2. Stretching	**Cool-down** 1. Skill contest 2. Stretching

Closure • Handouts • Talk with parents

> continued

SAMPLE SEASON PLAN, LEVEL 4 GIRLS *(continued)*

Week 7		Week 8	
Day 1	Day 2	Day 1	Day 2
Welcome • Warm-up • Attendance • Safety review • Practice agenda			
Warm-up 1. Jumping jacks 2. Conditioning 3. Basic stretching	**Warm-up** 1. Running 2. Conditioning 3. Basic stretching	**Warm-up** 1. Aerobic game 2. Conditioning 3. Basic stretching	**Warm-up** 1. Song and dance 2. Conditioning 3. Basic stretching
Vault 1. Running drills 2. Hurdle and rebound 3. Donkey kicks 4. Handstand on raised surface, fall to back 5. Handstand blocks and holds	**Floor** 1. Full floor routines 2. Work problem areas 3. Tumbling stations	**Beam** 1. Beam complex 2. Full beam routines 3. Make 5 of each skill	**Bars** 1. Full bar routines 2. Work problem areas 3. Strength
Beam 1. Beam complex 2. Full and half beam routines 3. Handstands: cross and side	**Bars** 1. Full and half bar routines 2. Make 5 of each skill 3. Strength	**Trampoline** 1. Jumps 2. Drops 3. Turns 4. Back saltos 5. Conditioning	**Vault** 1. Running drills 2. Hurdle and rebound 3. Donkey kicks 4. Handstand block to back 5. Handstand on raised surface, fall to back
Tumbling trampoline 1. Jump series 2. Front handsprings 3. Round off, back handspring, back handspring 4. Conditioning	**Vault** 1. Running drills 2. Jumping 3. Handstand blocks and holds 4. Forward roll onto mat stack 5. Handstand on raised surface, fall to back	**Floor** 1. Line drills 2. Full floor routines (back to back) 3. Work problem areas	**Beam** 1. Beam complex 2. Full beam routines 3. Work problem areas
Cool-down 1. Partner activity 2. Stretching	**Cool-down** 1. Fitness game 2. Stretching	**Cool-down** 1. Relay game 2. Stretching	**Cool-down** 1. Skill contest 2. Stretching
Closure • Handouts • Talk with parents			

© USA Gymnastics

Practice Plans

Coaches rarely believe they have enough time to practice everything they want to cover. To help organize your thoughts and help you stay on track toward your practice objectives, you should create practice plans. These plans help you better visualize and prepare so that you can run your practices effectively.

When developing daily practice plans, the first step is to consider how the flow of your practices will fit together over the course of one week. First, consider the limitations that may affect your plans: facility constraints, competitions, and other commitments that the gymnasts or other coaches may have. Many clubs have a full facility schedule allowing certain groups or teams to practice only on given days. Furthermore, some coaches may be able to help out only a couple of nights a week. Scheduling a level 4 team practice on Tuesday and Thursday evenings may look good on paper, but if you have no access to the vault or floor exercise, the plan will not be practical. It is likely that a coach would work together with the program director or club owner to carefully consider practice limitations and conflicts and set a weekly schedule.

Once you have a clear understanding of a weekly plan, the next step is to create daily practice plans. The flow of the daily practice plans should be designed so that the practice sessions fit together in a way that is not only practical but also maximizes the training effect. For example, a high-intensity and explosive workout that involves full routines on several events should be followed by a lower-intensity training session the next day. The day before a competition should be fairly low volume so that the gymnasts go into the meet rested. This will help them feel confident about their ability to do their best.

Remember that your daily practice plans should be age appropriate for the group you are coaching. The plans should incorporate all the skills and concepts presented in the particular age group's season plan. To begin, each practice plan should note the practice objective (which is drawn from your season plan) and the equipment necessary to execute the specific activities in the practice. Each practice plan should also include a warm-up and cool-down. During the cool-down, coaches should revisit any injuries suffered during practice and make sure the gymnasts drink plenty of water.

Following are two sample practice plans—one covering a week of practice for gymnasts at level 1 (page 228) and one for gymnasts at level 4 (page 231). You can use these sample plans as a guide when developing plans for your team.

Sample Lesson Plan, Level 1 Girls

Session 1, Week 1

Date: _____

Objective

The overall objective of the class is to introduce new students to basic gymnastics skills and provide a refresher for those who have participated in classes previously. We will focus on safety education, class rules, and developing a routine.

THEME/MUSIC

WARM-UP (5 MIN.)

Equipment
Part of the floor (or other carpeted or matted area)

Jumping Jacks

Half jacks

Regular jacks

Criss-cross jumps

Stretching

Neck: roll head from side to side

Shoulders: arm circles (forward and back, big and small)

Arms: shake out, cross in front and back, roll wrists

Trunk: twist from side to side, seesaw

Legs: lunge to one side and then the other, roll ankles

Body Positions

Tuck: tuck sit, squat

Pike: V-sit, pike stretch

Straddle: straddle stand, straddle sit

Straight body: straight stand, lying flat

Arch: on stomach

Hollow: on back, standing

Throughout the warm-up period, review class rules, structure, importance of the warm-up, and general safety rules. Also review safety rules for floor exercise.

FLOOR (15 MIN.)

Equipment
One-third of 40 by 40 ft (12 by 12 m) floor exercise mat (or carpeted or matted area)

Safe Landing Position

Review proper landing position and demonstrate. Have gymnasts practice position at the end of the floor after each exercise that follows.

Line Drills

Place all the gymnasts in a line across the floor. Gymnasts perform the movement the entire way across the mat.

Locomotions

　Walking in relevé (forward and backward)

　Side slide

　Bunny hop (forward and backward)

　Bear crawl

Basic Tumbling and Rolls

　Log roll (both directions)

　Tuck and straddle log roll (both directions)

　Forward roll (tuck)

　Forward roll to straight jump

　Straddle forward roll

　Back roll (use incline mats and spotting as needed)

BARS (15 MIN.)

Equipment

Single bar, low bar, single floor bar, wall bar, folded panel mats or block, parallettes, matted area, dial rod with weight

Safety reminder: How to come to the floor (dismount) to safe landing position. Review rules for bars.

Stations

Grips, hangs, pullover to forward roll dismount, strength (two to four repetitions per station, rotate through stations twice)

First Rotation of Station

1. Overgrip, undergrip, mixed grip (floor bar)
2. Straight hang (5 sec.)
3. Flexed arm hang (up to 5 sec.)
4. Pullover to front support, forward roll to dismount (spotted)
5. Support on parallettes (feet on ground)
6. Roll dial rod with weight
7. Leg lifts (five times) on floor
8. Prone plank hold (5 sec.)

Second Rotation of Station

1. Front support, lift one arm (floor bar)
2. Tuck hang (5 sec.)
3. Horizontal pull-up (two sets of five)
4. Support on parallettes (try to raise feet)
5. Dial rod roll with weight

> continued

Sample Lesson Plan, Level 1 Girls *(continued)*

6. Tuck-ups (five times) on floor
7. Lateral plank hold (5 sec. each side)

VAULT (15 MIN.)

Equipment
Vault runway, springboard, landing mat, skill cushion, low- and medium-height blocks, panel mats, stopwatch
Safety reminder: Safe landing position, safety rolls. Review rules for vault and pits.

Landing Drills

Jumps from medium-height blocks (or vault table) to correct landing position
Safety rolls

Running Drills

Running down vault runway or tumble strip
Normal run
Slow run, concentrating on arm movement
Fast run (timed)
High knees
Bottom kickers

Stations

Hurdles onto board, jumps off blocks, squat-on drills (four or five repetitions per station, rotate through stations twice)

1. Short run, hurdle onto board, rebound straight jump, freeze
2. Straight jump off low and medium blocks to freeze position (progress to tuck and straddle jumps)
3. Squat thrusts and squat on panel mat (moving down the mat)

COOL-DOWN (5 MIN.)

Partner Activity

Stretching

Shoulders: anterior shoulder stretch, partner chest stretch
Trunk: sit in straddle—stretch to one side, other side, center (chest down)
Legs: V-sit stretch, butterfly stretch, frog double, hamstring stretch, quad stretch

HANDOUTS AND ANNOUNCEMENTS

Safety handouts, coloring pages

Sample Lesson Plan, Level 4 Girls

Preseason, Week 1A

Date: _____

Objective

The overall objective of the class or team is to begin preparing gymnasts for level 4 competition by introducing and practicing the required skills on each event. Review team rules and safety considerations throughout the class.

WARM-UP (20 MIN.)

Equipment
Part of the floor (or other carpeted or matted area)

Jumping Jacks

Half jacks

Regular jacks

Criss-cross jumps

Conditioning

Tuck-ups

Plank holds (front, both sides)

Hollow body holds, arch holds (alternating)

Lunge walks

Leg lifts with wall bar (forward, backward, sideward)

Stretching

Neck: roll head from side to side

Shoulders: arm circles (forward and back, big and small)

Arms: shake out, cross in front and back, roll wrists

Trunk: twist from side to side, seesaw

Legs: lunge to one side and then the other, roll ankles and hip flexors

Back and shoulders: bridges

Throughout the warm-up period, review class rules, structure, importance of the warm-up, and safety rules.

FLOOR (30 MIN.)

Equipment
40 by 40 ft (12 by 12 m) floor exercise mat (or carpeted or matted area)
Safety reminder: Safe landing position. Review rules for floor.

> continued

Sample Lesson Plan, Level 4 Girls   *(continued)*

Line Drills

Place all the gymnasts in a line across the floor. Gymnasts perform the movement the entire way across the mat.

Locomotions

  Walking in relevé (forward and backward)

  Side slide

  Chassé

  Bunny hop (forward and backward)

  Bear crawl

  Crab walk

Rolls

  Log roll—straight, tuck, straddle (both directions)

  Forward roll (tuck, pike)

  Forward roll to straight jump

  Back roll (tuck, pike)

  Handstand forward roll (straight arms)

Cartwheels

  Right and left side

  Cartwheel-style round-off, rebound

Leaps, Jumps, and Turns

Gymnasts spread out around the floor. On the coach's command, gymnasts perform the skill in place. Repeat and provide feedback.

  Straight jump—step together, jump, proper landing

  Tuck jump

  Straddle jump

  Jump half turn

  Straight jump, tuck jump (in succession)

  Stride leap—straight legs, end in arabesque step forward

  Coupé turn—step forward on one foot and turn with free leg in coupé (half turn and full turn)

  Heel-snap turn—from stand in coupé, snap the heel around for half turn

Stations

1. Round-off, rebound
2. Round-off over mat stack
3. Bridge—push-up from floor, kickover (use incline mat if needed)

4. Bridge—stand up forward

5. Handstand over to bridge (use incline mat if needed)

BARS (30 MIN.)

Equipment
Single bar, low bar (two), single floor bar, wall bar, parallettes, matted area
Safety reminder: How to come to the floor (dismount) to safe landing position. Review rules for bars.

Stations

Pullovers, casts, back hip circles, squat ons, swing half turns, strength (four to six repetitions per station, rotate through stations twice)

First Rotation of Station

1. Jump to squat on, jump off forward (floor bar)

2. Flexed arm hand (10 sec.)

3. Pullover, forward roll to ground

4. Tuck support hold on parallettes

5. Casts (five in a row), return to bar

Second Rotation of Station

1. Squat on, jump off (single rail)

2. Tuck hang (10 sec.)

3. Swing half turn

4. L support hold on parallettes

5. Cast, back hip circle

VAULT (30 MIN.)

Equipment
Vault runway, springboard (two), Resi-Pit (or stacked mats with skill cushion on top), skill cushion, panel mats, stopwatch
Safety reminder: Safe landing position, safety rolls. Review rules for vault and pits.

Running Drills

Running down vault runway or tumble strip

Normal run

Slow run, concentrating on arm movement

Fast run (timed)

High knees

Bottom kickers

> *continued*

Sample Lesson Plan, Level 4 Girls *(continued)*

Hurdle and Rebound

Gymnasts take a few running steps to approach vaulting board. Hurdle onto board and rebound off. Perform designated skill or body position during rebound. Land in controlled position.

Straight jump

Tuck jump

Jump half turn

Straight jump to stacked mats

Stations

As for a circuit, take one turn at the station, and then move to the next. Continuous rotation.

1. Forward roll onto stacked mats—run, rebound from board to dive forward, roll onto mat stack (gymnast's waist height)

2. Handstand, fall to back—handstand onto vaulting board, block off to land in hollow position on skill cushion

3. Handstand hold—against the wall, slight hollow body, arms and shoulders completely extended (10 sec.)

COOL-DOWN (15 MIN.)

Partner Activity

Stretching

Shoulders: anterior shoulder stretch, partner chest stretch

Trunk: sit in straddle—stretch to one side, other side, center (chest down)

Legs: V-sit stretch, butterfly stretch, splits (right, left, middle)

HANDOUTS AND ANNOUNCEMENTS

Safety handouts, team rules, schedule

PLANS

Constructing practice plans requires both organization and flexibility on your part. Don't be intimidated by the amount of training you want to cover. Pick out a few basics, and build your initial practice plans around them; this process will get easier after you've drafted a few plans. Then you can move from teaching simple concepts and skills to drawing up plans that introduce more complex ones. Remember to include strength and flexibility. If you find that what you've planned for practice isn't working, you should have a backup activity that approaches the skill or concept from a different angle. The top priorities are to keep your gymnasts involved in practice and to help everyone have fun while they're learning.

Appendix

Related Checklists and Forms

This appendix contains checklists and forms. You may reproduce and use these checklists and forms as needed for your gymnastics program.

Please note that it is important to review all forms and checklists on an annual basis. All legal forms, such as waiver and release forms, should be evaluated by your local legal counsel and insurance agent to properly reflect your program and relevant state and local laws.

Coaches' Safety Checklist

USA Gymnastics recommends posting this information in the staff office or another place where it can be reviewed by staff before beginning daily activities.

Dress code (recommendation)

- ❏ Staff shirt neat, clean, and tucked in
- ❏ Athletic pants or shorts (professional in length)
- ❏ Athletic shoes or socks alone
- ❏ Hair neat in appearance and securely tied back
- ❏ Minimal or no jewelry

Properly plan the activity.

- ❏ Written daily lesson plans are important!
- ❏ Provide several stations to maximize activity time per event.

Provide adequate and proper apparatus and equipment.

- ❏ Before teaching an event, double-check the following:
  - Hardware used to tighten the apparatus is secure.
  - Mats are properly placed and secured (no gaps).
  - Obstacles are not in the vicinity of the activities.
- ❏ Ensure personal equipment fits properly and is used appropriately.

Know your students.

- ❏ Name
- ❏ Medical conditions
- ❏ Length of time in program
- ❏ Prior experience
- ❏ Skill level

Provide proper instruction.

- ❏ Regularly review falling and landing drills on each event.
- ❏ Review basic skills and positions.
- ❏ Teach with proper progressions.
- ❏ Provide safety education regularly.

Supervise *all* activities.

- ❏ Keep all your students within your field of vision.
- ❏ Reposition yourself or the piece of equipment or apparatus so you can oversee all students and activities.
- ❏ Use direct and indirect supervision as needed.

Keep adequate records.

- ❏ Lesson plans
- ❏ Progress reports
- ❏ Individual file per student
  - Incident report forms
  - Notes from parent or guardian
  - Medical information

Reprinted from *Gymnastics Risk Management: Safety Course Handbook*, page 110. © 2009 USA Gymnastics.

Safety Self-Audit Checklist

Administration of Gymnastics Activities

Safety Responsibilities

Are safety considerations, safety training, and safety experience included in job descriptions of the following positions?

1. Program administrators
2. Coaches
3. Athletic trainers
4. Instructors and teachers

Program Policies

1. Do policies exist concerning alcohol and drug use or abuse?
2. Do policies exist concerning supervision of athletes by coaches and instructors of the opposite sex?
3. Do policies exist concerning the disposition of athletes who are not picked up in a timely manner?
4. Are safety policies and procedures written and available to all relevant personnel?
5. Are facility inspections routinely scheduled and carried out?
6. Is a coach or instructor who is certified in first aid and CPR present at all gymnastics activities?
7. Are safety policies and procedures reviewed regularly?
8. Are equipment and apparatus needs regularly reviewed for safety?

Facilities

1. Is there a formal annual review of the condition of facilities and appropriate actions for maintaining or fixing the facilities?
2. Is there a designated person or persons responsible for facility inspections?
3. Are staffing plans available that ensure complete coverage of all gymnastics activities?
4. Is there a regular inventory of the facility and its contents?
5. Is access to the facility regulated and secured so that unauthorized use is not allowed?
6. Are special crowd-control policies available for public events?
7. Is signage clearly visible?
8. Is someone available to handle facility-related mishaps such as a spill or a broken piece of furniture?

Hazard Recognition and Inspections

1. Are inspection forms available and updated regularly?
2. Are facility inspections conducted regularly?
3. Are apparatus inspections conducted regularly?
4. Are equipment inspections conducted regularly?
5. When a hazard is discovered, is the hazard handled appropriately and quickly?
6. Are inspection reports filed appropriately?

> continued

Safety Self-Audit Checklist (continued)

Apparatus and Equipment

1. Is a formal review of all apparatus and equipment regularly conducted?
2. Is there a person who is responsible for the maintenance, repair, and replacement of apparatus and equipment?
3. Is a regular inventory conducted to determine the status of apparatus, equipment, and other disposables?
4. Are all participants, coaches, and instructors required to participate in an orientation regarding the safe use of new apparatus and equipment?
5. Does insurance cover all the apparatus and equipment in the facility?

Transportation

1. Are written policies available regarding who can drive to and from outside activities (e.g., qualifications)?
2. Are procedures in place to determine the credentials of drivers to and from outside activities?
3. Are those people with serious driving infractions excluded from driving?
4. Are certificates of insurance available for all transportation situations?
5. Is there a policy regarding the use of personal vehicles for transportation?
6. Are accident report policies established?

Employment

1. Are employment arrangements reviewed by an attorney?
2. Are attorneys consulted before discipline and before termination?
3. Can assistant coaches and instructors be terminated at will by the head coach?
4. Do arrangements specify various perks such as vehicles, tickets, summer camps, and so on?
5. Are coaches and instructors covered under the insurance of the gymnastics program?
6. Are coaches subject to a probationary period before final hiring?
7. Are prerequisite certifications, skills, background screening, and education specified before hiring?

Waivers and Releases

1. Are waivers required for participation?
2. Has the wording of the documents been reviewed by an attorney?
3. Do these documents conform to league rules and local statutes?
4. Are parental acknowledgments and release documents required?
5. Are consent documents for medical treatment available?
6. Are medical waivers readily available in an emergency?

Insurance

Do insurance and other policies cover the following:

1. Liability for all personnel
2. Property
3. Automobiles
4. Worker's compensation
5. Athlete medical
6. Coach and instructor medical
7. Volunteer medical
8. Medical malpractice
9. General liability
10. Employment
11. Fire

Use of Your Facilities by an Outsider

1. Are policies in place to determine who can use the facility and when?
2. Is there a contract or clear delineation of who is responsible for what?
3. Assuming a contract is needed, are policies in place to require insurance from the outsider?
4. Are there specific policies indicating who can approve outside use of the facility?
5. Are there specific policies indicating security measures that are required for a given use?
6. Are there specific policies to handle complaints, injuries, accidents, and so on?
7. Are there specific policies regarding coordination with emergency services for special use of the facility?

Injury and Incident Reporting

1. Do you confer with counsel regarding how to complete injury and incident reports and determine whether corrective actions are required?
2. Are injury and incident reports routinely reviewed by the program director?
3. Is there a procedure for implementing corrective actions after an injury or incident?
4. Do administrators, coaches, and instructors follow up after an injury to ensure that responses were proper and care was adequate?
5. Are emergency policies and procedures regularly reviewed?
6. Is there a regular meeting regarding safety and injury prevention?

Training

Coach and Instructor Training

1. Are coaches and instructors trained in safe techniques for their program area?
2. Are coaches and instructors trained in emergency procedures?
3. Are coaches and instructors trained in hazard recognition?
4. Are coaches and instructors trained in the use of emergency equipment?
5. Are coaches and instructors trained in reporting an injury or incident properly?
6. Are coaches and instructors trained to handle a catastrophic injury?
7. Are coaches and instructors trained to handle parents, spectators, and so on?

> continued

Safety Self-Audit Checklist (continued)

Participants

1. Are participants trained in proper techniques?
2. Has an attorney reviewed all relevant waivers, releases, consent to treatment forms, and other documents?
3. Are participants screened by a preparticipation self-assessment questionnaire or by a preparticipation physical examination?

Emergency Procedures

1. Are telephones and emergency numbers easily available?
2. Are suitable medical personnel available during events?
3. Are emergency transportation plans available?
4. Are consent to treatment forms signed and available?
5. Is at least one person trained in first aid and CPR present at all activities?
6. Are coaches and instructors trained in emergency procedures for extricating an injured athlete from a pit and from a trampoline?
7. Have emergency personnel been contacted regarding the special injury problems they will encounter in a gymnastics facility?
8. Have emergency personnel and program personnel practiced extrication procedures for athletes injured in a foam pit and in a trampoline?
9. Are policies in place to check credentials of medical personnel involved with the program?
10. Is the documentation appropriate for athlete participation examinations?
11. Are athletes and parents notified regarding the level of insurance coverage available to them in the event of an injury?
12. Are credentials checked for those responsible for rehabilitation services?
13. Is there a policy regarding when an athletic trainer or other personnel should be present at an event?
14. Are emergency procedures practiced?
15. Are policies available for contacting relatives of an injured athlete?
16. Is a well-equipped first aid kit available?
17. Is there a policy and plan for determining when heat and humidity require a reduction in training intensity or time?
18. Are fluids available for drinking at all times?

Attorney Review

1. Is counsel involved in drafting documents, reviewing policies, and reviewing injuries?
2. Has an attorney reviewed employment arrangements?
3. Has an attorney reviewed contracts that involve outside use of the facility?
4. In the event of a serious injury, has legal counsel been informed of the injury and previously planned how to deal with such an injury?

 Reprinted from *Gymnastics Risk Management: Safety Course Handbook*, pages 107-108. © 2009 USA Gymnastics.

Sample Facility Inspection Form

It is recommended that gymnastics club owners and program directors design a session or quarterly facility inspection form specific to their business. Inspection should be done by the owner, manager, or program director who is USA Gymnastics Safety/Risk Management certified. In addition, it is recommended that the apparatus and equipment be inspected by a representative from a reputable apparatus or equipment company.

For each item or area listed here, include the condition and any work required.

Date of inspection: _____   Time: _____

EXTERIOR

	Safe	Problems discovered and comments	Remedial action and date
Roof			
Gutters and downspouts			
Drain tiles			
Septic and sewer			
Exterior walls			
Paint and siding			
Doorways			
Sidewalks			
Trash and dumpster			
Parking			
Curbs			
Signage			
Entrance and exit signs			
Parking signs • Handicap parking • Handicap access • Delivery entrance			
Landscaping			

> continued

Reprinted from *Gymnastics Risk Management: Safety Course Handbook*, pages 103-105. © 2009 USA Gymnastics.

Sample Facility Inspection Form *(continued)*

INTERNAL

	Safe	Problems discovered and comments	Remedial action and date
Heating and cooling			
Emergency lights			
Gym lights			
Office lights			
Locker-room lights			
Stairwells and stairwell lighting			
Outlets			
Sound system			
Plumbing			
Toilets and urinals			
Showers			
Sinks			
Drinking fountains			
Fire sprinklers			
Office floor			
Gymnasium floor			
Exits visible and marked			
Fixtures padded			
Fire alarms working			
Fire extinguishers			
Flammable materials			
Cleaning materials			
Garbage cans			
Pro shop			

Reprinted from *Gymnastics Risk Management: Safety Course Handbook*, pages 103-105. © 2009 USA Gymnastics.

PROGRAM AREAS

	Safe	Problems discovered and comments	Remedial action and date
Dance studio			
Aerobics area			
Weight training			
Preschool area			
Classrooms			
Floor exercise			
Pommel horse			
Rings			
Parallel bars			
Horizontal bar			
Vault			
Uneven bars			
Balance beam			
Trampoline			
Double mini-trampoline			
Mini-trampoline			
Tumbling strip			
Tumbling trampoline			
Training pits			
Spotting belts			
Bungee cords			
Pulleys and ropes			
Signage			
Mirrors			

> continued

Sample Facility Inspection Form *(continued)*

GYMNASTICS APPARATUS AND EQUIPMENT

	Safe	Problems discovered and comments	Remedial action and date
Floor exercise • Clearance • Carpet • Foam • Rebound system • Mats • Signage displayed			
Pommel horse • Surface • T handles • Pommels • Base • Mats • Signage displayed			
Still rings • Ring frame • Cables • Turnbuckles • Straps • Floor plates • Mats • Signage displayed			
Parallel bars • Rails • Upright connections • T handles • Height adjustment • Mats • Signage displayed			
Horizontal bar • Rail • Height adjustment • Cables • Turnbuckles • Uprights • Floor plates • Mats • Signage displayed			

	Safe	Problems discovered and comments	Remedial action and date
Uneven bars • Rails • Height adjustment • Width adjustment • Cables • Cable tensioners • Turnbuckles • Uprights • Floor plates • Mats • Signage displayed			
Balance beam • Surface • Attachment to legs • Height adjustment • Mats • Signage displayed			
Vault • Surface • Attachment to legs • Height adjustment • Mats • Runway • Signage displayed			
Vaulting boards • Surface • Rebound system • Safety zone • Nuts and bolts • Springs • Signage displayed			
Trampolines • Mechanism for securing when not in use • Clearance • Springs • Frame • Frame pads • Bed • Spotting system • Signage displayed			

> *continued*

GYMNASTICS APPARATUS AND EQUIPMENT *(continued)*

	Safe	Problems discovered and comments	Remedial action and date
Mats • Stitching • Handles • Covers • Cushioning • Foam • Signage displayed			
Loose-foam training pits • Clean • Clearance • Edge padding • Bottom padding • Foam • Signage displayed			
Resi-Pits • Stitching and handles • Covers • Cushioning • Foam • Signage displayed			
Bungee system • Spotting platforms • Signage displayed			
Spotting belts • Stitching • Webbing • Buckles • Twisting belt movement • D rings and clips • Turning and support mechanisms • Signage displayed			
Overhead spotting system • Clearance • Ceiling clamps • Traveling cables • Ropes • Clips and swivels • Signage displayed			

Name of inspector: _____

Signature of inspector: _____ Date: _____

Reprinted from *Gymnastics Risk Management: Safety Course Handbook*, pages 103-105. © 2009 USA Gymnastics.

Sample Registration Form
With Waiver and Release

NOTE: Legal forms should be reviewed annually and must be evaluated by local counsel in light of applicable state laws. Always consult with an attorney before using this or other forms.

Participant Registration Form

Before participation in any activity, this form must be signed by at least one of the participant's parents or legal guardians if the participant is not yet 18 years old. The participant's signature is required if 18 years of age or older and is helpful when age appropriate.

Participant's name: _____   Male / Female: _____

Age: _____   Date of birth: _____

Mother's name: _____   Father's name: _____

Legal guardian's name: _____

Address: _____

City: _____   State: _____   Zip: _____

Phone: (___) _____ Cell: (___) _____ Emergency: (___) _____

E-mail address: _____

Are there any medical conditions we should be aware of?   __ Yes   __ No

  If yes, explain: _____

Has the participant had a physical examination in the last three years? __ Yes __ No

  _____ [insert gymnastics club's name] recommends that every student complete an annual physical examination.

Physician's name: _____   Phone: (___) _____

Dentist's name: _____   Phone: (___) _____

May we use the gymnast's photo on our Web site or in advertisements? No names will be disclosed.   __ Yes   __ No

Eligibility to participate in class at _____
[insert gymnastics club's name] requires a completed gymnast registration form with release of liability, a consent to treatment form, and full tuition on or before the first day of class.

_____   _____
Gymnast   Date

> continued

Sample Registration Form
With Waiver and Release *(continued)*

If gymnast is not yet 18 years old, *at least one* parent or legal guardian of said person must also sign:

We certify that the information provided here is correct.

_____	_____	_____
Printed name of parent or guardian	Signature of parent or guardian	Date
_____	_____	_____
Printed name of parent or guardian	Signature of parent or guardian	Date

LIABILITY RELEASE AND INDEMNIFICATION: Before participation, this form must be signed by at least one of the participant's parents or legal guardians if the participant is not yet 18 years old. The participant's signature is required if 18 years of age or older and is helpful when age appropriate.

Name of participant (the "gymnast"): _____ DOB: _____

Address: _____

Home phone: _____ Alternate phone: _____

Name of parent or guardian (print): _____

Name of other parent or guardian (print): _____

In consideration of _____'s [insert gymnastics club's name] allowing the gymnast to participate in sports activity, class, competition, and team, including nongymnastics activities such as dance, cheerleading, swimming, and playground activities (hereinafter referred to as the "activity"), I, and if I am not yet 18 years old, my parents or legal guardians, agree to be bound as follows (the term *I* in this release refers to both the gymnast and his or her parents or legal guardians):

1. **Acknowledgment and assumption of risks.** I understand that the activity involves risks of serious bodily injury, including permanent disability, paralysis, and death, which may be caused by the gymnast's actions or inactions, those of others participating in the activity, the conditions in which the activity takes place, the negligence of the released parties named below, or other causes. I further understand that there may be other risks either not known to me or not readily foreseeable at this time. I fully accept and assume all such risks and all responsibility for losses, cost, and damages that may result from the activity. I hereby give my approval of and consent to the gymnast's participation in the activity. I assume all risks and hazards incidental to the activity and to transportation to and from the activity.

2. **Representation of ability to participate.** I understand the nature of the activity, and I represent that the gymnast is qualified, in good health, and in proper physical

condition to participate in the activity. Should I ever believe that any of the above representations have become untrue, or if I should ever believe that the activity is not safe or is no longer safe for the gymnast, then it will be my responsibility to immediately discontinue the gymnast's participation in the activity.

3. **Release.** I hereby release, acquit, covenant not to sue, and forever discharge _____ [insert gymnastics club's name], its owners, officers, administrators, employees, agents, volunteers, sponsors, advertisers, coaches, and supervisors and the owners or lessors of any facilities within which the activity is conducted, their respective agents and employees, and all other persons providing facilities or assisting in the conduct of the activity and in the transportation of participants to and from the activity (collectively the released parties) of and from any and all actions, causes of actions, claims, demands, liability, losses, or damages of whatever name or nature, including but not limited to those arising from or in any way related to the negligence of any of the released parties, that arise out of or are connected in any way to the gymnast's participation in the activity and the transportation of the previously named gymnast to and from the activity (collectively the released claims).

4. **Indemnification.** I will defend, indemnify, and hold harmless the released parties from (that is, to reimburse and be responsible for) any loss or damage, including but not limited to costs and reasonable attorney's fees (including the cost of any claim I might make or that might be made on my behalf or the gymnast's behalf that is released in this document), arising out of or connected in any way with any of the released claims.

I have read the policies and procedures for parents, spectators, and participants in the activity or team handbook and agree to abide by all rules and conditions set forth therein and to accept the judgment of the program officials in this regard.

I HAVE READ AND UNDERSTOOD THIS ACKNOWLEDGMENT AND ASSUMPTION OF RISKS, REPRESENTATION OF ABILITY TO PARTICIPATE, RELEASE, INDEMNIFICATION, AND CUSTODIAL PARENTS. I UNDERSTAND THAT BY SIGNING THIS DOCUMENT, I AM GIVING UP SUBSTANTIAL RIGHTS. I AM EXECUTING THIS DOCUMENT VOLUNTARILY AND WITH FULL KNOWLEDGE OF ITS SIGNIFICANCE.

_____	_____
Gymnast	Date
_____	_____
Signature of parent or guardian	Date
_____	_____
Signature of other parent or guardian	Date

Sample Incident Report Form

Attach additional pages if necessary.

NOTE: Legal forms should be reviewed annually and must be evaluated by local counsel in light of applicable state laws. Always consult with an attorney before using this or other forms.

Date of report: _____ Date of incident: _____ Time: _____

Person involved in incident (circle one):

Gymnast   Instructor/Coach   Spectator   Other: _____

Name: _____ Age: _____ Gender: _____

Address: _____

City: _____ State: _____ Zip: _____

Home phone: _____ Other phone: _____

Level: _____ Club: _____

Emergency contact: _____ Phone: _____

Incident:

Site of incident (if not club): _____

Location or event where incident occurred: _____

Activity, apparatus, and equipment involved: _____

Full description of incident, including injured body part: _____

_____

Has this problem occurred before?   Yes   No   Unsure

Action taken, including first aid or other treatment: _____

_____

Witness:

First name: _____ Last name: _____

Address: _____

City: _____ State: _____ Zip: _____

Home phone: _____ Other phone: _____

OFFICE USE ONLY

Person making report: _____ Person in charge: _____

Director's acknowledgment (date): _____

Owner's acknowledgment (date): _____

Follow-up call (date): _____

Follow-up information: _____

ATTACH A COPY OF PHYSICIAN'S RELEASE

NOTE: If this incident occurred at a USA Gymnastics–sanctioned event, an accident insurance report form must also be completed and sent to USA Gymnastics' insurance provider.

Reprinted from *Gymnastics Risk Management: Safety Course Handbook*, page 106. © 2009 USA Gymnastics.

Sample Consent to Treatment Form

NOTE: Legal forms should be reviewed annually and must be evaluated by local counsel in light of applicable state laws. Always consult with an attorney before using this or other forms.

Before the athlete participates, this form must be signed by at least one of the participant's parents or legal guardians if the participant is not yet 18 years old. The participant's signature is required if 18 years of age or older and is helpful when age appropriate.

Name of participant:_____ (the "gymnast") DOB: _____

Address: _____

Home phone: _____ Alternate phone: _____

Name of parent or guardian (print): _____

Name of other parent or guardian (print): _____

In consideration of _____'s [insert gymnastics club's name] allowing this person to participate in sports activity, class, competition, and team, including nongymnastics activities such as swimming and playground activities (hereinafter referred to as the "activity"), I, and if I am not yet 18 years old, my parents or legal guardians, agree to be bound as follows (the term *I* in this release refers to both the gymnast and his or her parents or legal guardians):

I authorize _____ [insert gymnastics club's name] to provide to the participant, through medical personnel of its choice, customary medical assistance, transportation, and emergency medical services should the gymnast require such assistance, transportation, or services as a result of injury or damage related to participation in the activity. If the gymnast is a minor and a parent or guardian is not present, efforts will be made to contact a parent or guardian that are reasonable under the circumstances, but treatment will not be withheld if a parent or guardian cannot be reached. The parent's or guardian's phone number is as follows: _____.

Please provide the following information regarding the participant:

Participant's personal physician: _____

Doctor's phone: _____

Doctor's address: _____

Participant's medications: _____

Participant's allergies: _____

Participant's significant medical history: _____

Primary medical insurance carrier and policy #: _____

I also affirm that I now have and will continue to provide proper hospitalization, health, and accident insurance coverage that I consider adequate for the participant's protection. This consent shall remain effective until one year from the date below unless sooner revoked in writing and delivered to _____ [insert gymnastics club's name and address].

I HAVE READ AND UNDERSTOOD THIS CONSENT TO TREATMENT AND AM EXECUTING THIS DOCUMENT VOLUNTARILY AND WITH FULL KNOWLEDGE OF ITS SIGNIFICANCE.

_____   _____
Gymnast   Date

_____   _____
Signature of parent or guardian   Date

_____   _____
Signature of other parent or guardian   Date

Reprinted from *Gymnastics Risk Management: Safety Course Handbook*, page 111. © 2009 USA Gymnastics.

Emergency Information Card

Athlete's name: _____   Sport: _____

Age: _____

Address: _____

Phone: _____

Provide information for parent or guardian and one additional contact in case of emergency.

Parent's or guardian's name: _____

Address: _____

Phone: _____

Other phone: _____

Additional contact's name: _____

Relationship to athlete: _____

Address: _____

Phone: _____

Other phone: _____

Insurance Information

Name of insurance company: _____

Policy name and number: _____

Medical Information

Physician's name: _____

Phone: _____

Is your child allergic to any drugs?   Yes   No

   If so, what? _____

Does your child have any other allergies (e.g., bee stings, dust)? _____

Does your child have any of the following?   Asthma   Diabetes   Epilepsy

Is your child currently taking medication?   Yes   No

   If so, what? _____

Does your child wear contact lenses?   Yes   No

Is there additional information we should know about your child's health or physical condition?   Yes   No

   If yes, please explain: _____

Parent's or guardian's signature: _____   Date: _____

 From American Sport Education Program, 2011, *Coaching youth gymnastics* (Champaign, IL: Human Kinetics).

Emergency Response Card

Be prepared to give the following information to an EMS dispatcher. Note: Do not hang up first. Let the EMS dispatcher hang up first.

Caller's name: _____

Telephone number from which the call is being made: _____

Reason for call: _____

How many people are injured? _____

Condition of victim(s): _____

First aid being given: _____

Location: _____

Address: _____

City: _____

Directions (e.g., cross streets, landmarks, entrance access): _____

_____

Glossary

amplitude—External amplitude is the height or distance an element is performed away from the apparatus. Internal amplitude refers to proper alignment or body positioning during the performance of an element.

arch—The upper and lower parts of the back are stretched backward, forming a curve.

artistry—The ease of movement, quality of expression, and aesthetic performance of skills, links, and choreography exhibited throughout a routine.

assemblé—Pushing off one foot while swinging the other leg forward and up, bringing the feet together upon landing.

backbend—From a stand, arching backward to place the hands on the floor to form a bridge.

back handspring—A move where a gymnast takes off from two feet, jumps backward onto the hands, and flips over to land on the feet; also known as a flic-flac or flip-flop.

balance—A static position that holds a distinct shape.

blocking—To "spring" off the hands by putting weight on the hands and using a strong push from the shoulders. Blocking is a critical component of front handspring-type skills and most vaults.

bridge—An arched position with the feet and hands flat on the floor and the abdomen up. This position is achieved by lying on the back and pushing up onto the hands and feet.

butterfly stretch—While sitting on the floor, bending the knees and bringing the soles of the feet together so the knees go out to the sides. The gymnast should try to touch the knees to the floor.

cat leap (pas de chat)—Jump forward off one leg while swinging the other leg forward and up, switch leg positions in midair, and land on the takeoff foot. Legs are bent at 90 degrees during flight.

compulsories—Predesigned routines that contain specific skills and movements required of all gymnasts.

coupé—Standing on one leg, the free leg bent and toes pointed, with the big toe at the ankle of the support leg. Knee (of free leg) can face forward or sideward.

crab stand—A flat, tabletop-like position with feet and hands flat on the floor and abdomen up. Hips should be open and torso extended and parallel to the floor. This is a skill progression for a bridge.

dismount—A skill performed from the apparatus to a controlled landing on a mat.

dynamic—A skill or movement showing flight.

element—A single move or skill that has an expected standard of execution and has been given a technical value.

execution—1. The performance of a routine. 2. The form, style, and technique used to complete the skills included in a routine.

flexibility—The range of motion through which a body part, such as the shoulders or legs, can move without feeling pain.

fouetté—Pushing off one leg while kicking the other leg forward and up, executing a 180-degree turn, and then landing on the first leg. The other leg remains extended back.

front attitude—Standing on one leg, the free leg lifted forward so the thigh is horizontal, and turning the leg out, with the knee bent slightly.

front support—Arms are straight and extended in front of the body. This is also known as a plank or push-up position.

gymnastics point (tendu)—Beginning with a stretched body position, placing one foot forward with the leg straight, toe pointed and lightly touching the floor. The other leg should remain straight and support the body weight. The hips are square. This is often used as a starting position for gymnastics skills.

handstand—An inverted position with hands flat on the floor, shoulder-width apart, and the body completely extended and straight, legs together.

hand to hand—A partner balance skill in acrobatic gymnastics where the top partner is in a handstand position supported by one or two hands of the base partner.

hitch kick—Pushing off one leg while swinging the other leg forward and up, switching leg positions in midair, and landing on the other foot. Legs are extended.

hollow—Beginning from a stretched body position, contracting the chest and abdomen inward with a pelvic tilt and bringing the shoulders forward. Gymnast should have a rounded upper back.

hurdle—A long, low, powerful skip step that may be preceded by one or more running steps. Generally used to generate power into a round-off tumbling series. Also used as an approach onto a rebound device, such as a vaulting board, mini-trampoline, or double mini-trampoline.

inverted—Any position in which the lower body is moved into a position above the upper body, such as a handstand.

kip—A move from a position below an apparatus to a position above it. Kips are often performed on uneven, parallel, and high bars.

layout—Also called straight or stretched position. Usually performed as a body shape in a salto.

leg circles—A standard pommel horse move where a gymnast keeps the legs together and swings them in a full circle around the horse, with each hand lifted in turn from the pommel to let the legs pass.

lunge—Position in which one leg is forward and flexed, and the other leg is straight and extended backward. The body is stretched and upright, with weight over the front leg. A lunge is often used as an initiation or finish position for gymnastics skills.

mount—A skill performed from the floor to get onto an apparatus. This is typically the first skill in a routine.

optional—The design of the routine and skill selection is determined by the coach and gymnasts. Gymnasts portray their best skills while meeting the requirements of the level of competition. Routines can be constructed to reflect the gymnasts' strongest abilities.

pancake—A stretch performed in a straddle sit. The gymnast leans forward to touch the chest to the floor and extends the arms in front or to the sides to touch the ankles.

passé—Standing on one leg, the free leg bent and toes pointed, with the big toe at the knee of the support leg. Knee (of free leg) can face forward or sideward. The thigh (upper leg) of the free leg should be horizontal.

pike—The body is flexed forward at the hips while the legs remain straight.

pirouette—A term used to describe a turn on one leg, a turn in handstand position, or a turn in the air while executing a jump.

pivot—A sharp turn or quick change in direction, typically performed as a quarter or half turn on two feet.

plié—Bending the knees with feet flat on the floor and the body straight and upright. Demi-pliés (slight bend of the knees) are important for safe landings and takeoffs. Depending on the skill, the legs, knees, and feet may be turned out or facing forward.

prone—Lying facedown on the floor.

rear support—Arms are straight and extended behind the body.

rebound—A quick jump using very little flexion of the hips, knees, or ankles.

relevé—Standing in a straight position on the balls of the feet (on toes).

routine—Multiple skills or series linked together. Another term for a routine is *exercise*.

salto (somersault)—A skill where the lower body rotates over the upper body. It can be performed backward, forward, and sideward.

scissors—A skill performed on the pommel horse that combines cuts and undercuts. It begins in a stride support and ends in an opposite stride support.

series—Two or more skills performed consecutively. Can also be called a sequence.

sissonne—Jumping from two feet (one foot in front of the other), separating legs into a split position in the air, and then landing on the forward foot. Can also be done to the side and back.

split—Position where the legs are extended to 180 degrees. Can be done as a stride (straight) split or a straddle (middle) split.

spot—Physically guiding or assisting a gymnast who is performing a skill. Spotting is a helpful tool in the learning process.

squat—Support on the balls of the feet with the knees and hips flexed so that the buttocks is near, but not touching, the heels and the torso is erect.

stick—Slang for when a gymnast executes a landing with correct technique and no movement of the feet.

straddle—A position in which the legs are straight and extended sideward.

straight stand—Standing with the feet together, either parallel or turned out 45 degrees, legs straight, abdomen tight, rib cage lifted, arms at sides, and head neutral. When the arms are extended up by the ears, this position is called a stretched stand. Body should form a straight line.

stride leap—Pushing up and forward off of one foot to travel forward and land on the opposite foot, showing flight with legs in straight (or stride) split position.

supine—Lying flat on the back.

tuck—The body is curled up in a ball. The upper body is flexed forward and flexed at the hips, and the knees are flexed and pulled up to the chest.

upper arm swing—A move on parallel bars with the upper arms resting on the rails to provide support while the body swings through the bars.

walkover—A move from a standing position through a handstand position back to a standing position while "walking" through the air with the feet.

About the Authors

USA Gymnastics is the sole national governing body for gymnastics in the United States, with more than 98,000 athletes registered in competitive programs as well as more than 20,000 professional, instructor, and club members. USA Gymnastics, through its Professional Development Program, is dedicated to providing gymnastics coaches and instructors with the best coaching and teaching information available today.

Content expert **Kathy Feldmann,** vice president of membership services at USA Gymnastics, has been involved in gymnastics for over 40 years. She has been a high school and college coach, physical education and health teacher, and private gymnastics club owner. Currently she holds a brevet rating as a women's gymnastics official. Before assuming her current role, Kathy held positions in the USA Gymnastics organization as a national, regional, and state chair. She has been a USA Gymnastics collegiate liaison, commissioner of officials for Massachusetts high schools, delegation leader for World Championships in 1994, and team leader for World University Games in 1995, 1997, and 1999. Kathy judges competitions for the Junior Olympic level as well as the collegiate level. She has officiated at numerous national, Olympic Trials, and international events. She was a technical assistant official at the 1996 Olympic Games in Atlanta.

Kathy has been at the USA Gymnastics national office since 1997. As vice president, she oversees the three divisions of membership, club services, and educational services. She is the director of the annual national congress and trade show, which is the largest educational event conducted by USA Gymnastics.

Loree Galimore (director of club services) and Carisa Laughon (former director of educational services) contributed to the writing and development of this book.

Loree Galimore is a former gymnast, club owner, and coach and is a national women's gymnastics judge. She has worked with USA Gymnastics since 1996 and is now the director of club services. She helps people with the business of gymnastics, provides industry statistics, and markets the sport of gymnastics.

The **American Sport Education Program (ASEP)** has been developing and delivering coaching education courses since 1981. As the nation's leading coaching education program, ASEP works with national, state, and local youth sport organizations to develop educational programs for coaches, officials, administrators, and parents. These programs incorporate ASEP's philosophy of "Athletes first, winning second."